W9-CDA-983

Connecticut's War Governor:

Jonathan Trumbull

By **DAVID M. ROTH**

A Publication of
The American Revolution Bicentennial
Commission of Connecticut

Published by

P E Q U O T   P R E S S

Chester, Connecticut

1974

ISBN: 87106-149-X
Library of Congress Catalog Card Number: 74-82316
Manufactured in the United States of America
All Rights Reserved

FIRST PRINTING

Contents

Governor Jonathan Trumbull (1710-1785) and Mrs. Jonathan (Faith Robinson) Trumbull (1718-1780).

The Making of the Man

THERE are men whose fiber appears to be of their own invention. Such men appear to be children of no age or place. There are others, however, perhaps most of the race, whose mature years, like a stream constantly churning up pebbles from the bed beneath, consistently reflect the physical and philosophical characteristics of their youthful environment. Such a man was Jonathan Trumbull. Whether one views him as a husband, father, public figure, or merchant, Trumbull's essential nature was related to the world of his boyhood in Lebanon, and throughout his mature life, he was never to be completely free from the early forces which molded his character—Puritan theology, the Protestant ethic, and the personality of his father.

Jonathan Trumbull was the younger son of Joseph Trumbull who moved from a none-too-successful farm in Simsbury, Connecticut, to the developing town of Lebanon in 1705.[1] Joseph, who was characterized by his artist-grandson, John Trumbull, as a "respectable, strong minded but uneducated farmer,"[2] promptly demonstrated in Lebanon that drive and ambition which were to be reflected so clearly in the life of his son Jonathan. The elder Trumbull purchased land with a "modest dwelling house," and in a short time he had expanded his agricultural opeations to include trading. Focusing on raising cattle in Lebanon and buying additional stock in neighboring towns, Joseph Trumbull drove the cattle to Boston where he accepted payment in English manufactured goods which he was able to dispose of in Lebanon in a substantial retail trade.[3]

Joseph Trumbull was soon able to translate his economic success into significant public recognition. A member of the First Ecclesiastical Society since 1705, he became a lieutenant of the Windham County Troop of Horse in 1718, captain in 1728, and quartermaster in 1730.[4] Thus, although not enjoying the advantages of a formal education and having come from rather inconclusive beginnings in Simsbury, Joseph Trumbull's energy and ambition, coupled with the social fluidity of the early Connecticut Valley, permitted him to establish a firm base in Lebanon for his two sons, Joseph, Jr., born in 1705, and Jonathan, born on October 12, 1710.

The Lebanon in which Jonathan Trumbull grew to manhood was a town just emerging from the frontier stage of development. Although first settled around 1697 and allowed to send representatives to the Connecticut General Assembly in 1705, the town showed no significant population growth until the early 1730s.

The area was one which undoubtedly demonstarted to young Jonathan Trumbull the necessity of sustained labor as a basis for

5

achievement. The land clearing, the fence building, the road construction, and the constant care of field and stock were activities which played a major role in the boy's early years.[5] The undeveloped and agrarian nature of early Lebanon thus inspired in Trumbull a realization that man's task was to strive and to contribute. There was no such thing in his environment as success achieved without effort. The very perpetuation of the individual and the family was linked directly to the completion of those physical tasks which constitute the central core of existence in an essentially agrarian society. The lesson, no matter how conveyed, was effective, for Trumbull, both as a merchant and especially as a public figure, would be characterized by a truly amazing capacity for work.[6]

Trumbull's commitment to labor was further reinforced by the Puritan spirit which dominated Connecticut society during the years of his youth. Connecticut, more than any place on earth in the early eighteenth century, approached the spirit and structure of the Wilderness Zion. While the original Puritan zeal in old England had long since waned and the strident Calvinism of Massachusetts had deteriorated to a detectable secularism, Connecticut held scrupulously to the doctrines of Thomas Hooker's generation.

Connecticut Puritanism, unthreatened by external political or cultural intrusions, succeeded in maintaining itself as the *raison d'etre* of the society through the first third of the eighteenth century. The Connecticut Calvinist interpreted his mission as unchanged from that of his seventeenth-century forefathers who had entered the Connecticut Valley after a short migration from Massachusetts Bay. Thomas Hooker reasserted the Puritan charge which had previously been given classic statement by John Winthrop aboard the *Arbella* in 1630. Winthrop had admonished one of the early Puritan contingents in his "A Model of Christian Charity" to labor to complete the Protestant Reformation by bringing forth a society that would be cleansed of the impurities which the Calvinist saw flourishing in England under the Anglican Church.[7] Hooker explained clearly the route that the individual was to follow if the new settlement were to succeed in its holy charge:

> So, I would have you do, loose your selves . . . and all that you have, and do, in the Lord Christ. How is that? Let all be swallowed up, and let nothing be seen but a Christ . . . As it is with the Moon and Stars, when the Sun comes, they lose all their light, though they are in the heavens still. . . . So let it be with thy Soul, when thou wouldest find mercy and grace.[8]

Nor could the Puritan of Connecticut abandon the idea that man's nature was essentially corrupt. If man were to lose himself in Christ, as Hooker put it, he required the support, if not frequently the coercion, of an institutional structure founded upon and committed to

God's word.[9] Thus, the Connecticut Puritans promoted the establishment of a social order which would reinforce the ideological basis of the society.

The founders of Connecticut evolved and maintained a system in which each individual was to contribute to the realization of the Puritan mission. Ethical standards, sexual mores, educational patterns, and, of course, religious observances were all comprehensively controlled. Never in Puritan society was the inclination of the individual to take precedence over the aspirations of the community. Society to the Puritan was not an aggregation of individuals. It was an organism in which all parts were subordinate to the whole. The individual had as his primary responsibility that of contributing to communal success. He was to obey the elders, to live within the confines of God's word, to educate his children so that they might in the future sustain the society, and to do that labor to which he was "called" by God.[10]

Jonathan Trumbull thus grew to manhood in an environment still permeated by Puritan thought and practice. While he undoubtedly had the release afforded by the popular children's games of the day, and while rural Lebanon must have presented him with opportunities to enjoy swimming, hunting, and fishing, his youthful enthusiasm was tempered by strict parental and communal religious direction. Daily prayers were to be said. The Scriptures were to become the root of his conduct. He was to approach his responsibilities with the unquestioned conviction that what was at stake was nothing less than the salvation of his eternal soul and the Christianization of the world.

It would have been difficult to foresee in the early 1720s, however, that young Jonathan would spend his mature years in business and politics, for Joseph Trumbull, Sr., had clearly intended the boy for the Congregational ministry. Since the elder son, Joseph, Jr., was immersing himself in the family agricultural and trading operations and Jonathan had manifested a taste for scholarship, the younger son had been given over to the town pastor, the Reverend Samuel Welles, for college preparation. When Jonathan was thirteen, in 1723, he was sent to Harvard to prepare for the Congregational ministry. Even here, Joseph Trumbull, Sr., was clearly revealing his continuing concern for the social advancement of the family, for the Trumbull star, already bright with the thriving Lebanon mercantile activity, could only be made more intense in the reflection of a young Puritan divine.

Arriving in Cambridge with the class of 1727, and being ranked thirty-fourth in a class of thirty-seven, Trumbull set about his college studies. While the young man from rural Lebanon must have been stimulated by his academic fare and at least excited by the more sophisticated Boston atmosphere, Trumbull appears to have gone through his college years without experiencing any discernible intellectual ferment. No sparks were struck; no new conceptions were perceived which might have caused the youngster to rethink his personal values and assumptions. Rather, it would seem that Trumbull's Harvard career, as was true of every successive stage in his life, brought no inclination to redefine either his own nature or that of his environment.

Jonathan Trumbull thus went about his academic labors at Harvard with no marked enthusiasm for his studies, and, not surprisingly, achieved no significant academic distinction. The only unique aspect of Trumbull's Harvard career was an action which indicated his persistent religious consciousness. In his first year at Cambridge, Trumbull joined the "Private Meeting," a religious society which had been organized in 1719. The articles of this organization revealed the intense religious focus of the members:

> It being our indispensable Duty as well as undeniable Interest, to improve all Opportunities, and Advantages that God is graciously favoring us with, to his Honor and Glory, and our eternal welfare, as also to avoid all those Temptations and Allurements to Evil, which we are in danger to meet with, and to Edife, encourage, and excite one another in the ways of Holiness, and Religion. . . .[11]

Following commencement in 1727, Trumbull returned to Lebanon. He then read theology with the local parson, the Reverend Solomon Williams, and returned to Harvard in 1730 to take his M.A. with his class, his thesis being that there were no contradictions in Scripture which could not be solved by reason.

In 1730, he took the covenant in his church and was licensed to preach by the Windham Congregational Association. In June, 1731, he received an invitation from the Colchester congregation to assume the pulpit. While considering and perhaps preparing for what would have been his first professional appointment, Trumbull found his plans altered by the first of the many personal tragedies he was to experience.

Joseph Trumbull, Sr., and Joseph Trumbull, Jr., along with several others from Lebanon, either constructed or purchased a brigantine which was called the *Lebanon*. The vessel, with Joseph Trumbull, Jr., on board, sailed on December 29, 1731, from New London bound for Barbados and Sal Tortuga. Neither the vessel nor Joseph Trumbull, Jr., was heard from again, and it was soon presumed that the *Lebanon* had foundered at sea.[12]

As the months passed with no word from Joseph, Jr., Jonathan was called upon by his father to help with the family business. Acceptance of the call from Colchester had, of course, to be deferred. As the months lengthened into years with continued silence about the fate of his brother, Jonathan Trumbull found himself fully immersed in the family firm, Trumbull and Son.

The death of Joseph Trumbull, Jr., was thus a most significant turning point in the life of Jonathan Trumbull, but one can all too easily overestimate its importance in Trumbull's life by assuming that the vocational alteration brought a decisive change in the character of the man. Such was not the case.

Trumbull was not one who took only figuratively the Winthrop admonition to bring forth the "City upon a Hill." Throughout his life, Trumbull seemed to function on the basis of the Puritan assumption that man did God's work no matter what one's vocational condition might have been. All that the individual achieved was related to the individual's regeneration as well as to the evolution of a truly godly society. Thus, it mattered little to the Puritan whether one occupied God's pulpit, anguished over that sterile New England soil, or bore the burdens of the mercantile maelstrom. All was the same if it were done in the service of the Lord. Therefore, although he exchanged the pulpit for the marketplace, and later the political chamber, the man never experienced a diminution of his religious orientation.

It might perhaps be said that Trumbull's immersion in secular concerns upon the death of his brother gave him the opportunity to manifest the ambitiousness which he seemed to have inherited from his father. Trumbull, as was true of so many of his Puritan forefathers and peers, could sincerely devote himself to achievement in the name of individual and communal regeneration and at the same time focus upon the satisfaction of his own not inconsiderable vanity. Throughout his life, he would never lose sight of the main chance, the decision which would clearly bring the greatest glory to the name and estate of Trumbull. It was perhaps this trait which motivated Trumbull's political enemies to conclude that his religious commitment was but a socially-acceptable cloak behind which he hid his blunt ambitiousness. Yet, although the charge might have given some comfort to his critics, the evidence does not indicate that it was true. Jonathan Trumbull was no hypocrite. He was a man, like many a Puritan, one suspects, who accepted a theological code which called for a superhuman diminution of self, but, being just a man, was not capable of eschewing earthly prizes. He was a man with a deep-seated religious orientation, a sincere commitment to the concept of service to one's fellows and to God, and, as well, an unmistakable vanity which was not often disregarded throughout his life. As might be said of so many Puritans, so it might be said of Trumbull: his imperfections were large only in light of the towering nature of the life style he sought to serve.

The Puritan, subject as he was to an "interminable high seriousness" and an unquestioned conviction that he was doing the work of the Lord, was not, after all, an individual who could often accept the existence of nuance or alternate modes of thought. The Puritan saw not only just the black and the white; he was intellectually incapable of recognizing that a gray might exist. God's writ to the Puritan was clear and bold, and there was no conceivable justification for tampering. Trumbull approached life with just such a conviction. As he faced momentous political decisions, Trumbull did not experience any soul-wrenching indecision. He reacted to the political issues of his era with an instinctual certainty which was incompatible with the views of others. Such righteousness was undoubtedly a spur to resolute leadership; it was also the reason why Trumbull was to be so detested by his political opponents.

Lebanon Merchant

JONATHAN's entrance into Trumbull and Son was dictated by the need of Joseph Trumbull, Sr., to have the help of his surviving son in operating the business. Either because of the great competence of the son or the father's failing health, however, within four years, Jonathan Trumbull had completely taken over the conduct of the family firm.[1]

The first phase of Jonathan Trumbull's mercantile career, from the early 1730s to 1744, was one in which Trumbull could be categorized most accurately as an inland merchant, i.e., one who did not conduct any importing business from overseas but who relied upon coastal merchants for both the disposal of the goods he was producing and the purchase of manufactured goods from abroad.

The backbone of Trumbull's business—as it had been of his father's—was the provisions trade in both livestock and packed meat. Trumbull's usual outlets for barreled provisions were in Boston, Newport, Providence, Norwich, and New London.

This meat trade provided the capital required to carry on the second phase of his mercantile operation—the distribution of goods and supplies in the area surrounding Lebanon. Purchasing "sundry" manufactured goods in Boston, Trumbull shipped them by water to Norwich where he frequently bought salt and sugar. He then transported the merchandise to retailers in many of the towns in which he purchased his cattle and hogs.

The final aspect of Trumbull's business activities was his retail trade within Lebanon itself. As the principal shopkeeper in a rural and isolated community, Trumbull had to carry an inventory that was broad enough to satisfy all retail demands. He dealt, therefore, in a bewildering variety of goods—pepper, lace, gloves, gunpowder, flints, molasses, rum, drugs, paper, cord, pails, needles, knives, indigo, log-wood, earthenware, raisins, thimbles, buckles, tea, buttons, combs, butter, spectacles, soap, brimstone, nails, and pewter dishes, to name but a few.

Given Trumbull's important economic standing, as well as the economic and social position his father had established, it is not sur-prising that the energetic Harvard graduate soon entered political life. In 1733, the young merchant had been elected as the town deputy to the Connecticut General Assembly.[2] Although he failed of election in 1734 for reasons unknown, Trumbull regained his seat in the General Assembly in 1736.[3] From that time, Trumbull was to be a constant, and increasingly significant, figure in Connecticut political life. His public distinctions in these early years also included local military and judicial appointments. In 1735 he was appointed to the rank of lieuten-ant in the Troop of Horse of Windham County and was made a lieu-tenant colonel in the Twelfth Connecticut Regiment in 1739.[4] His judicial career began in 1738 with his appointment as justice of the peace and quorum for Windham County.[5]

Trumbull's rise in the 1730s reveals much, regarding both the nature of the society and the man. The recognition Trumbull received indicates the existence of vertical social mobility in early eighteenth-century Connecticut. Jonathan, representing the second generation of Trumbulls in Lebanon, was not only able to surpass the rank of his father, but, as indicated by his election to the General Assembly, to become perhaps the major figure in the community. Both father and son were able to capitalize on the area's social fluidity because their conduct reflected the qualities honored by the community—wisdom, industry, courage, and, above all, that sense of piety which was rooted in the Congregational establishment.[6]

On December 9, 1735, after a "brief courtship,"[7] Jonathan Trum-bull married Faith Robinson, the daughter of the Reverend John Robinson of Duxbury, Massachusetts, and a direct descendant of no less than John and Priscilla Alden. Faith Robinson Trumbull proved to be a woman whose quality was apparent to all,[8] but Trumbull never escaped the charge that his marriage was based upon his desire to strengthen the family name. Trumbull *had* made a marriage that was socially advantageous, a consideration that was not lost upon those who later were to score Trumbull as a clever opportunist who had carefully charted his course toward social and political recognition. Trumbull's Tory critic, Samuel Peters, commented:[9] "His marriage with this lady . . . raised him from obscurity to a state of nobility; for all who have any blood in their veins of the first settlers . . . are considered in New England as of the rank of Noblesse. Mr. Jonathan's matrimonial connections . . . [gave] him the prospect of preferment in civil life."

Reaping the rewards of his own ambition and the social fluidity of early eighteenth-century Lebanon, Trumbull in the 1740s was a man who appeared to have a rather comprehensive grasp of success. Yet, there were some clouds on the Trumbull horizon. There appeared an element in his business situation which would ultimately bring him to almost complete financial collapse. Trumbull's ledgers showed in 1741 that he was owed over £5000 by his retail customers.[10] Such a situation was not, on the surface, extraordinary, when one recognizes that eighteenth-century New England economic life revolved to a considerable extent around credit.[11] Trumbull's cattle trade in and around Lebanon was largely carried on without the use of cash. He would usually pay for his cattle purchases with goods bought from him throughout the year by the cattle sellers. Although the coastal importing merchants, especially in Boston, normally required cash payments for the goods Trumbull sought, in 1741, he owed such men over £3000. Business transactions on a credit basis, then, were not unusal. But what was unique about Trumbull's financial condition in the early 1740s was that the debts that he owed to the importing merchants were fresh. These debts had to be paid quickly if Trumbull were to receive additional goods. Debts owed to him by his local customers, on the other hand, were long-standing, and were, for the most part, not collectable.[12]

Trumbull, like most retailers in an area such as Lebanon, followed a liberal credit policy with respect to his customers. He often accepted payment in such items as livestock, tobacco, firewood, flaxseed, lime, feathers, cranberries, beeswax, grain, turnips, potatoes, malt, and furs. Nor was it unusual for him to permit his customers to discharge their financial obligations to him by such services as carting, farm labor, carpentry jobs, and mason work.[13] In allowing his customers to build up debts of over £5000, however, Trumbull had exceeded liberality to the point of foolishness.

What accounted for Trumbull's granting of excessive credit? The ready explanation is that perhaps Trumbull, recognizing, as he undoubtedly did, the scarcity of specie in rural Lebanon, was simply a victim of compassion for his fellow townsmen. Such an explanation has perhaps a certain validity to it, but, unfortunately, evidence exists to bring Trumbull's mercantile compassion into question.

Settlers from Massachusetts Bay and Connecticut, including some from Lebanon, had gone to settle in Nova Scotia in 1760 and 1761 after the British had expelled the "Acadians" in 1755. For the most part, these migrants had a most difficult time. They found upon arriving that the soil required substantial work to fit it for cultivation. Too, they found that a number of homes had either been burned at the time of the expulsion of the French or had deteriorated into a dilapidated condition. A final blow to the expectations of the settlers was a severe drought which put many of them in a hopeless financial state. Trumbull was one of the Connecticut merchants who responded to the desperate need of these people for provisions. He did not, however, display much generosity, for he drove an extremely hard bargain by exacting mortgages on land in Connecticut and Nova Scotia in exchange for the provisions.

A more likely explanation of his liberality regarding credit is the type of "image" which Trumbull sought to create of himself in the community. Ambitious, as we have seen, Trumbull adopted a life style that was characterized by lavish hospitality at his home on the Lebanon Green and by minute attention to the quality of his possessions.[14] Such a man, obviously bent on projecting himself as the local "merchant prince," perhaps found it difficult to establish his position among his "subjects" while at the same time dunning them for nonpayment.

Such an explanation of Trumbull's liberal credit policy takes on added validity when one notes the somewhat questionable status of merchants in eighteenth-century America. They were regarded, especially in rural, agrarian areas, as parasites who drained the community. Farmers saw merchants as a "set of sharpers, who are constantly on the watch for plunder and gain," as men who proved by their consumption of rich wines and exotic spices that their appetites were "too delicate to relish the natural productions of their country."[15] Recognizing the existence of such attitude, and realizing that its application to him would obviously detract from the social and public recognition he had sought, it is not unlikely that Trumbull concluded that dunning his fellow townsmen would never do.

No matter what the exact reason for Trumbull's liberal credit policy, it is clear that by the early 1740s it had put him in an unfortunate predicament. His ledgers bulging with debts owed to him that in some cases went as far back as 1735, he faced the pressing demands for payment from the importing merchants with whom he dealt. Trumbull's position, however, was strengthened by side ventures which brought him considerable income. The operation of his farm, flour mill, malt house, brewery, and fulling mill, although time-consuming, brought him additional funds which could be applied to his payments to the coastal merchants. Nevertheless, such additional income was not sufficient to get Trumbull even, particularly because he continued, despite all logic, to grant his retail customers excessive credit. In fact, by 1762, the money due him exceeded £10,000! Between the 1740s and 1760s, while his personally-destructive liberal credit policy continued, Trumbull sought desperately for a finanical panacea which would shore up his deteriorating condition. Although he went about his quest with his usual energy, it proved to be essentially fruitless.[16]

During King George's War (1744-1748), Trumbull and Hezekiah Huntington, a Norwich merchant, were given a contract in the summer of 1746 to supply the Connecticut men preparing for an invasion of Canada with "flintlocks, cutlasses, cartouchboxes, and belts."[17] By the late 1740s, Trumbull had formed a partnership with Elisha Williams of Wethersfield and Joseph Pitkin of Hartford to import manufactured goods from Britain. While the firm of Trumbull, Williams, and Pitkin was in existence until the death of Elisha Williams in 1755, Trumbull explored various routes to cure his financial ills. He, along with his partners, received over £6,000 worth of merchandise from Samuel Sparrow, a London merchant; opened up an account with another London merchant, Thomas Lane; entered the Nantucket whale-oil trade; exchanged provisions for British manufactured goods with Joshua Mauger of Halifax; and explored a plan to send masts to Britain for the Royal Navy.[18] And finally, during the French and Indian War (1754-1763), Trumbull became involved in army provisioning. In 1756, he was one of the merchants who furnished provisions for the Connecticut expedition to Lake George. Also, in 1761, Trumbull and Hezekiah Huntington were charged by the General Assembly to provide the 2,300 Connecticut troops in the field with "refreshments and clothing."[19]

As the English-speaking world celebrated the Treaty of Paris of 1763, Trumbull could take pride in the fact that he was one of the major figures in "His Majesty's Colony of Connecticut." He had become the pivot around which the community of Lebanon revolved. Following the death of his father in 1755, Jonathan made Joseph Trumbull, Sr.'s residence the center of local social life. He had, moreover, become a major force in the area's intellectual development. In 1738 he had been one of the organizers of an early American non-academic library, the Philogramatician Society of Lebanon.[20] The birth of his children—Joseph (1737), Jonathan, Jr. (1740), Faith (1743), Mary (1745), David (1752), and John (1756)—led Trumbull to cooperate with his townsmen in the establishment of a grammar school in Lebanon in 1743. The school under Nathan Tisdale gave Trumbull's children their early education and in time became, according to John Trumbull, "the best school in New England."[21]

Trumbull's influence by the early 1760s transcended the confines, further, of his native Lebanon. At Harvard, where students were "placed" according to the status of their family, young Joseph Trumbull of the class of 1757 was ranked third, while his brother Jonathan, Jr.

14

of the class of 1759 was ranked first. The elevated status that the Trumbull young men enjoyed at Harvard was a clear reflection of the father's position as a major merchant, as the premier citizen of Lebanon, and as a principal figure in Connecticut government. By the early 1760s, Trumbull had become a fixture in the colony's governing apparatus. He served in the General Assembly, except for one year, as either a deputy in the House of Representatives or as an assistant in the council throughout the 1740s and 1750s.[22] He was the man whom the Assembly consistently turned to when faced with crucial tasks, such as representing the colony at intercolonial conferences during King George's War and the French and Indian War.[23] His judicial responsibilities expanded as well in these years as he served in Windham as justice of the peace and judge of the county and probate courts.[24] In 1754 he declined an appointment as an assistant judge of the Connecticut Superior Court.[25] During the French and Indian War, although not serving in the field, Trumbull was made colonel of the Twelfth Connecticut Regiment.[26]

Trumbull, then, could well in 1763, at age fifty-three, take pride in his substantial achievements. Yet, the tragedy of Jonathan Trumbull's situation in the 1760s was that he had little time to savor his accomplishments. Bankruptcy was about to dash his business career, for Trumbull, despite his hectic business activity in the 1740s and 1750s, found himself in the 1760s still the victim of his foolish credit policy. Throughout his mercantile career, Trumbull generally was able to secure an adequate supply of manufactured goods which he was able to sell at a fair profit. Such advantages did him little good, however, because the products sold appeared as debts in his ledgers rather than as cash in the drawer. By the 1760s, with the colonies suffering a trade depression following the French and Indian War and merchants on both sides of the Atlantic calling in their debts, Trumbull found himself in an impossible plight. Faced with insistent demands to pay up from merchants in Boston, New York, and London, Trumbull's ability to meet his obligations was exasperatingly frustrated by his lack of success in collecting some £10,000 owed to him by his specie-starved customers in Connecticut[27]

As Trumbull evaluated his situation, the Lebanon merchant was confronted with the necessity of making a fundamental decision. In short, Trumbull had to choose between giving up the ghost of his business and declaring bankruptcy, or attempting to remain in trade as long as possible with the expectation that a financial *coup* might enable him to pay his debts. Having recognized the intense vanity of the man, it is perhaps understandable that Trumbull would not follow the former course. The humiliation of bankruptcy would have been devastating to the Trumbull who had labored a lifetime to establish himself as Lebanon's first citizen. Gone would be the lavish hospitality at the Trumbull home, the fine carriage, the quality clothing made in Boston from imported English fabrics, and undoubtedly, that elevated social ranking which the family had come to enjoy. Such losses might have been accepted by some. They were, however, too terrifying for Jonathan Trumbull even to consider.

The path, then, that Trumbull would take regarding his declining business was clear. He would try, throughout the 1760s, to hang onto the last remnants of solvency while he desperately sought a business arrangement that would prove lucrative. During almost each year of the decade, he would explore some new mercantile avenue to shore up the crumbling Trumbull financial structure. At the same time, his attention would be diffused by the effort necessary to keep his creditors at bay. From Boston, from New York, but especially from London, the man was inundated by increasingly shrill demands for payment. No one, of course, can accurately estimate what this experience did to Jonathan Trumbull. A glimpse of his agony is, however, discernable in his mercantile correspondence during these years. The backs of scores of his letters are filled with endless lists of figures, indicating that he sat day after day calculating interminably over figures which always led to the same depressing conclusion—his business was in ruins.[28]

In 1763 or 1764, Trumbull entered into a partnership with his son Joseph and Eleazer Fitch of Windham, a man who had become wealthy through dealings in land and trade. Joseph journeyed through Britain in 1763-1764 exploring various mercantile opportunities, and Fitch's capital enabled Trumbull to again secure manufactured goods from English merchants.[29] The existence of the firm of Trumbull, Fitch, and Trumbull enabled Jonathan Trumbull to continue in business and at the same time to hold off his creditors with descriptions of the profits the new partnership would reap. Yet, all came to naught. A series of collapsed plans and business losses was too much for the new firm to bear. Eleazer Fitch withdrew in 1767, and Trumbull, Fitch, and Trumbull was dissolved. Jonathan Trumbull was in the most desperate stage of his business career. He was without any apparent means of conducting his business, and he was faced with the thoroughly legitimate demands of creditors who had been more than patient with him. Neither the association with Fitch nor Joseph's arrangements had brought Trumbull any financial benefit. Having absolutely no prospects in sight, Trumbull could have taken with honor only one path—bankruptcy.

Trumbull, however, chose to take another route. Obviously ridden by that vanity which was his constant characteristic, unwilling or incapable of witnessing the erosion of his public and social position which bankruptcy would have brought, Jonathan Trumbull embarked upon a delaying action. From 1767 until the outbreak of the Revolutionary War, Trumbull used every weapon at his disposal to thwart the justifiable demands made upon him by his creditors.[30] To men who as a group had treated him with remarkable understanding and patience, Trumbull returned evasions and, when possible, contempt. Using his office of deputy governor from 1766 to 1769 and of governor after 1769, Trumbull sought to either dodge or intimidate his creditors. Trumbull indeed was able to avoid bankruptcy; that, however, is the only positive assertion one can make of his conduct during this critical phase of his business life.

Political Apprenticeship, 1736-1763

T RUMBULL's entrance into the House of Representatives as the deputy from Lebanon in 1736 signified little concerning his potential for political responsibility. His election was simply a reflection of his economic and social standing in an unimportant agrarian town in eastern Connecticut. Further, the mere fact of his continuing tenure in the house and later in the council was no more revealing concerning his substantive political abilities. Continued public service in the first half of the eighteenth century in "the land of steady habits" meant only that an individual supported the standing social and religious order and had not embarrassed either himself or his community by unseemly conduct.[1] The Connecticut Wilderness Zion was ruled by the leading lights of the Puritan Establishment, and an individual of some religious substance upon entering public life could naturally expect to be re-elected for as long as he wished to bear the burdens of public office. Thus, a man with Trumbull's known commitment to the Standing Order could have managed to establish such a record of public service with no more ability than that of avoiding fatal illness.[2]

The extraordinary feature of Trumbull's public service, however, was that it was anything but that of a phlegmatic backbencher who hung on in government year after year only on the basis of religious and social respectability. After a little more than five years service in the House of Representatives, Trumbull in 1740 at age thirty had risen to the post of speaker.[3] The distinction, further, was but the first of many he was to earn in the next decades. As the Connecticut General Assembly met its major responsibilities between 1740 and the Treaty of Paris, it was Trumbull who was consistently called upon to handle the crucial assignments.

One of the facets of Connecticut life over which the General Assembly exercised jurisdiction was that of religion.[4] The essentials of worship in eighteenth-century Connecticut had been provided for the Assembly in 1708 by its adoption of the Saybrook Platform. Drawn up by the colony's Congregational ministers, the code provided for the support of a centralized Congregational Establishment, even by those Connecticut residents who were not members of a Congregation. The discipline of the church was to be enforced by Consociations of churches and Associations of ministers throughout the colony.[5]

But there were significant complications which precluded religious harmony in Connecticut. As Connecticut's population went from 38,000 in 1730 to 130,000 in 1756,[6] tightly-ordered communities, especially in Connecticut's sparsely-settled eastern area, expanded, inevitably raising questions regarding ecclesiastical jurisdictions between the original and the developing parishes.[7] The conflicts over jurisdiction were exacerbated in the period by the appearance of substantial numbers of dissenters such as Baptists, Quakers, and Anglicans, and this influx helped to weaken the ecclesiastical and theological solidity of the Congregational Establishment.[8] Finally, Connecticut was shaken alarmingly by the explosion of the Great Awakening in the 1740s. Exploiting the decline of religious interest, which was a common result of eighteenth-century American secularization, evangelical preachers such as George Whitefield raged throughout the colony calling for a return to the simple piety of past generations.[9] The "New Lights," those who came to support the evangelical appeals of men such as Whitefield, found themselves in conflict with the "Old Lights," those who rejected the emotional excesses and the separatist inclinations of the revivalists.[10]

Charged with the supervision of the colony's religious life, the General Assembly from the 1740s to the 1760s was hard pressed to preserve even minimal ecclesiastical stability. The most common problem confronting the Assembly was that of a congregation which sought to be divided into smaller separate units on the basis of doctrinal or geographical considerations. When faced with an application seeking mediation in the proposed division, the Assembly usually appointed a committee composed of deputies or assistants who had some knowledge of the area in which the parish was located. Jonathan Trumbull was the man the Assembly used most consistently to deal with religious divisions and disagreements in such towns as New Concord (1738-1739), New London (1739), Killingly (1741), Mansfield (1743-1745), Norwich (1748), Middletown (1749-1750), Saybrook (1750), Kensington (1753), Plainfield (1760), and Windham (1760-1761).[11]

The General Assembly found Trumbull to be a responsible member in areas other than that of ecclesiastical mediation. No man in the colony was delegated more regularly to represent Connecticut in inter-colonial affairs than was the Lebanon merchant. One Assembly charge given to Trumbull was to represent the colony in the 1740s regarding a boundary dispute with Massachusetts. Connecticut and the Bay Colony had been at odds for a century over the location of Connecticut's northern boundary. The two colonies attempted unsuccessfully to resolve the issue in 1642, 1649, 1695, 1702, 1713, 1716, and 1724.[12] By the 1740s, the principal point of contention was whether the towns of Woodstock, Suffield, Enfield, and Somers were to be under the jurisdiction of Massachusetts or Connecticut. In 1747, the towns petitioned the General Assembly, seeking incorporation into Connecticut.[13] The Assembly appointed a committee of Jonathan Trumbull, John Bulkley, Benjamin Hall, and Roger Wolcott to meet with representatives of Massachusetts to resolve the matter.[14] Massachusetts, probably recognizing that she had nothing to gain from talks with Connecticut but the possible loss of the four towns, refused to negotiate. Connecticut finally acted in 1749, when the General Assembly voted to accept the four towns and again appointed Trumbull to serve on a committee to meet with delegates of the Massachusetts General Court.[15] Massachusetts continued to ignore the Connecticut General Assembly. Undaunted, the Assembly once more in 1750 delegated Trumbull, Bulkley, Wolcott, and Joseph Fowler to treat with Massachusetts.[16] The Bay Colony continued to pout regarding the matter until 1800 when it ceased any longer to complain of Connecticut's incorporation of the four border communities.[17]

The Connecticut General Assembly, as it had in peace, turned to Trumbull in time of war. In 1744, the Anglo-French struggle for North America re-erupted with the outbreak of King George's War. In February, 1745, the Connecticut General Assembly dispatched Trumbull and Elisha Williams to Boston to take part in a conference on intercolonial strategy against the French. The principal concern at the meeting was the daring scheme of Governor William Shirley of Massachusetts for an assault on the French fortress of Louisbourg on Cape Breton Island. Trumbull and Williams must have reported favorably on the prospects for success, for upon their return to Connecticut the Assembly pledged to contribute to the effort some five hundred men under the command of Deputy Governor Roger Wolcott.[18] Trumbull continued to represent Connecticut in strategy conferences in Boston in the summer of 1746. In both June and August, at meetings of the intercolonial planning board, Trumbull repeatedly urged that New York and Rhode Island involve themselves in the conflict to the extent that Connecticut and Massachusetts had done.[19]

As the Anglo-American world girded itself in the mid-1750s for what would be the decisive stage in the conflict with the French,

Trumbull once again came to be Connecticut's principal delegate to intercolonial strategy meetings. Trumbull and Ebenezer Silliman were sent by the Assembly in November, 1755, to New York to attend a planning conference,[20] and in January, 1756, Trumbull and Phineas Lyman went to Boston to confer with Shirley regarding the proposed attack on Ticonderoga and Crown Point.[21] Connecticut responded to the plan on which Trumbull reported by calling out over 3,000 men for the campaign of 1756.[22] The next year saw Trumbull meeting in Boston with the new British commander-in-chief, Lord Loudoun.[23] Once again, the Connecticut General Assembly demonstrated trust in the military operations Trumbull had helped to plan by calling out close to 1,500 troops for use against Louisbourg and Fort William Henry.[24] Trumbull concluded his service in intercolonial planning during the French and Indian War by attending two meetings in 1758. In January, he met in Boston with royal and colonial delegates to implement Pitt's energetic vision of assaults on Louisbourg and on Canada *via* Ticonderoga and Crown Point.[25] Further plans for the operations were made at an intercolonial conference in Hartford in March, with Trumbull, Ebenezer Silliman, and William Wolcott serving as the Connecticut delegates.[26] Connecticut shouldered a major share of the troop and provisions commitment for the assault on Canada, which, in 1759, culminated in Wolfe's dramatic capture of Quebec.[27]

While Trumbull's service in King George's War and the French and Indian War reveals clearly the extent to which he was respected by his fellow members of the General Assembly, perhaps his service for the colony in the Spanish Ship Case in the 1750s indicates even more precisely his position in Connecticut public life. This episode centered on the cargo of the *Saint Joseph and Saint Helena*, a Spanish snow on a voyage from Honduras to Cadiz, which sprang a leak at sea and put into the port of New London in November, 1752. The vessel had a rather lush cargo of forty chests of silver, one chest of gold and over 500 bags of indigo, all of which was valued at 400,000 Spanish dollars, and conflict took place between Joseph Hull, the British customs collector of New London, and Gurdon Saltonstall of New London who was appointed by Governor Wolcott to oversee the valuable cargo while the vessel was being repaired. Additional complications came when the agent for the vessel was set upon for huge claims for payment by those in New London who had been responsible for the salvage and repair of the vessel. As though the situation were not sufficiently messy, an inventory of the cargo revealed that a number of the chests had been looted of the specie, which had been replaced by stones and sand.

The agent for the vessel, Joseph Miquel de San Juan, who, by the way, had also been fleeced by two New York attorneys whom he had employed to contend with the machinations of the New London salvage and repair people, had, not unexpectedly, reached the end of his rope. He wrote to Governor Wolcott: "I believe without doubt, . . . that either your Honor, the royal official [Hull], or the province, ought to make good all the damages, thefts, delays and time lost, which follow on this business. . . ." San Juan's blast had the effect of rather promptly sobering the people of Connecticut, who, it must be said, took rather comic delight up to this point in the difficulties the unloved Spanish were having. Now, however, it appeared that the colony might have to bear the financial responsibility for the losses of the Spanish snow. Not surprisingly, public opinion went against Governor Wolcott for not having handled the matter with more dispatch and precision, and the result was that the next election in April, 1754, saw Wolcott turned out of office, as Thomas Fitch, the incumbent deputy governor, was elected to the governorship.[28]

While the voters of Connecticut had their revenge in the humiliation of Wolcott, the colony was not going to be able to avoid responsibility for the losses of the Saint Joseph and Saint Helena quite so easily. This fact became clear when the "Governor and Company of Connecticut" heard from the British government in June, 1754. Sir Thomas Robinson, Secretary of the State for the Southern Department, criticized Connecticut for not having protected the cargo; noted that a British man-of-war, the Triton, under the command of Captain Whitwell, was coming to New London to oversee the dispatch of the cargo to Spain; and concluded: "It being his Majesty's most Serious Intention (which I cannot help repeating to you in the Strongest manner) that the Court of Spain shall have the fullest Justice and Satisfaction imaginable."[29]

Governor Fitch and his council, justifiably alarmed that Connecticut might well find itself pressured by both London and Madrid for damages to the Spanish, set up a committee to cooperate with Captain Whitwell. The committee would have as its task not only the job of preparing the cargo of the Saint Joseph and Saint Helena for shipment to Spain, but even more taxing, that of convincing Captain Whitwell, and through him the British and Spanish governments, that the colony was doing everything possible to deal with a difficult situation. Connecticut turned for the performance of this complicated assignment to Jonathan Trumbull and Roger Wolcott, Jr.[30]

Trumbull and Wolcott introduced "a most refreshing efficiency" into Connecticut's conduct in the case. They first set about making an inventory of the cargo, and found that the Spanish had lost some forty bags of indigo, 5,000 Spanish dollars in gold, and about 15,000 Spanish dollars in silver. The remaining cargo was promptly loaded aboard ship, and when the vessel sailed from New London in January, 1755, Captain Whitwell acknowledged that Trumbull and Wolcott had cooperated fully.[31]

Connecticut, however, was not yet out of the woods. Secretary Robinson wrote to the colony in November, 1755, that the Spanish government was not satisfied that justice had been done it, claiming that it sought the part of the cargo that had been retained in Connecticut. The British government responded to the Spanish pressure by dispatching to New London in May, 1756, a man-of-war to collect the remainder of the cargo of the *Saint Joseph and Saint Helena*. Once again, Connecticut turned to Jonathan Trumbull and Roger Wolcott, Jr., to cooperate with the British. They joined the British captain, Charles Proby, in an investigation of the affair, and put together a deposition that made it clear that recovery of the missing cargo was not likely. Although Connecticut heard once more in 1758 from London that the Spanish were still complaining to the Court of St. James, Jared Ingersoll, then the Connecticut agent in London, was able to report in 1761 that the matter had been dropped by Madrid.[32]

Less dramatic than his services to Connecticut in the Spanish Ship Case were Trumbull's efforts in the 1740s and 1750s in overseeing the colony's finances. In 1742, 1743, 1744, 1745, 1747, 1749, 1751, 1752, 1754, and 1755 Trumbull served on the committee of the General Assembly to audit the colony's accounts in the possession of the treasurer and to report to the Assembly.[33] During both King George's War and the French and Indian War, he served on special committees of the Assembly to draw up the colony's expenses in preparation for reimbursement claims to London.[34] Finally, in the 1730s and 1740s, when Connecticut was shifting from old to new tenor bills of credit, Trumbull was charged by the Assembly to lend such portions of the issue as were not needed for the colony's immediate use.[35]

Jonathan Trumbull of Lebanon, then, was a pivotal figure in Connecticut government from the 1730s to the 1760s. During the 1740s and 1750s especially, he was the Connecticut public figure who was charged by the General Assembly to handle the most taxing assignments. Among Trumbull's discernable assets were the solid nature of his constitution and his unrivaled capacity for work. No matter how laborious or time-consuming the task, Trumbull was consistently able, year after year, to bear the emotional and physical burdens. Trumbull's physical sturdiness and his unimaginative intellectual outlook may not have made of him a dramatic or romantic figure; they assuredly, however, made him a man of unbreakable solidity.

Trumbull's political prominence was due, then, to more than simply his availability. He clearly must have impressed his fellow members in the General Assembly with his absolute reliability. The

Puritan-Yankee mentality which dominated the Connecticut Zion not unexpectedly placed great emphasis upon fiscal soundness. Although Trumbull's personal financial difficulties in the 1760s would perhaps detract from his public image, in the 1740s and 1750s the fact that he was charged with persistent fiscal responsibilities reveals the extent to which he was viewed as utterly dependable. Besides auditing the colony's accounts, preparing financial statements dealing with Connecticut's wartime expenditures, and overseeing new currency issues, Trumbull was appointed in 1754, with John Ledyard and Elihu Chauncy, to "inquire into the state of the treasury, and endeavor to bring the Treasurer's accounts into good form," or essentially to establish a new system of bookkeeping for the colony's accounts.[36]

Perhaps the foremost characteristic which was revealed in Trumbull's political conduct in the 1740s and 1750s was a remarkably temperate or judicious approach to controversy. A great many of the tasks delegated to Trumbull involved mediation among various interests, and he must have demonstrated a relatively even disposition and the ability to contribute to the achievement of a viable consensus among diverse points of view.

Most indicative of the careful path which Trumbull trod was the position he assumed regarding the "New Light"-"Old Light" issue. On the one hand, Trumbull was generally regarded in Lebanon as sympathetic to the simple piety and earnest zeal of the evangelicals. For Trumbull to take such a position was politically productive, when one notes that eastern Connecticut was the heartland of the revivalist impulse. Yet, strong opposition to the "New Lights" existed in western Connecticut and was expressed in the General Assembly.[37] Not surprisingly, Trumbull was responsible in the General Assembly for the introduction of legislation in 1743 which was strongly "Old Light." The bill of 1743, called "one of the most reactionary pieces of legislation in New England history," was a potent "Old Light" measure which struck at revivalism by prohibiting preachers, even those ordained by the Congregational Establishment, from entering a parish without invitation.[38] Trumbull was clearly not consistent in his supporting, at the same time, "New Light" piety in Lebanon and the bill of 1743 in the General Assembly; he was, however, most successful in retaining the good will of both the "New Lights" and the "Old Lights."

Another indication that Trumbull in these decades did not lose sight of considerations of personal advancement was his response to the General Assembly when he was asked to become Connecticut's agent in London. Requested to accept the post in March, 1756, he replied:

I have carefully weighed the matter, and acknowledge my obligations in gratitude to serve my country in whatever lies in my power, considering every relative duty; and as nothing but a sense of such obligation to duty would be any inducement for me to undertake that important and arduous trust, so a sense of my own insufficiency for that service pleads my excuse; and when I consider the duties I owe to my aged mother, whose dependence is greatly upon me, and all the circumstances of the case, I think I may conclude that I am not negligent or undutiful when I decline the service, and desire the Honorable Assembly to turn their thoughts on some other person.[39]

Upon being asked once again to serve in the post in May, 1758, he once again declined:

On serious and mature consideration—that I have not had the small pox—. . . and that it is at all times frequent in London—the circumstances of my family—I think it fit and reasonable not to accept and undertake the important Trust of an Agent for this Colony at the Court of Great Britain, unto which, at this time, you have done me the honor of an appointment. With a grateful sense of this further expression of your confidence, which I hope never to forfeit, and an humble reliance on your Candor and excuse, I shall ever pray for the Blessing and Direction of the Almighty and all-wise God in your Counsels.[40]

While the excuses Trumbull gave to the Assembly were substantial, it is likely that additional considerations contributed to his decision. One such consideration was that the London post would at best have brought Trumbull a niggardly salary. More importantly, Trumbull's ambitions could more likely be satisfied by remaining in Connecticut. He undoubtedly hoped to become involved in army provisioning during the French and Indian War with financially beneficial results.[41] Finally, the agency in London would lead to but a considerable absence from Connecticut, after which Trumbull might indeed find that others had assumed his eminent position in the colony's government. A man of Trumbull's ambition was hardly going to allow three decades of services to be forgotten while he toiled away forgotten across the Atlantic.

Trumbull and the Coming
of the Revolution

PARLIAMENT'S passage of the Sugar Act in 1764 and the Stamp Act in 1765 evoked a negative response throughout Connecticut.[1] Yet, western Connecticut, softened in its attitude toward the mother country by its economic ties to the royal colony of New York and by the work of Anglican missionaries in the decades before the Revolution, was inclined to limit its reaction to reasoned declarations of protest. Eastern Connecticut, on the other hand, having seen its economic and religious inclinations frustrated for over thirty years by a General Assembly dominated by western Connecticut, vented its accumulated hostility upon the British legislation and the "westreners" who were portrayed as "soft" on the imperial issue.[2] Forming the Sons of Liberty to rally opinion against both London and the "westerners," eastern Connecticut led a sweeping denunciation of the Stamp Act. The hard line of the "easterners" was manifested most dramatically in the intimidation of Jared Ingersoll in September, 1765, and in the meeting of the Connecticut Council of Assistants of November 1, 1765, when Governor Thomas Fitch was prepared to take the oath required of all American governors to execute faithfully the provisions of the Stamp Act.

In one of the most memorable scenes in early Connecticut history, Governor Fitch entered the chamber and explained to the council that he intended to take the required oath. Although opposed to the principle of taxation inherent in the Stamp Act, Fitch reasoned in a manner acceptable to the western-Connecticut viewpoint that Americans had no choice but to accept the legislation. Having made his decision, Fitch was thus forcing the members of the council to make fundamental decisions of their own, and each of them, including Jonathan Trumbull of Lebanon, would have to resolve whether he would meet his responsibility by administering the oath to Fitch. The question was, of course, momentous, since refusal to participate in the ceremony would render a councillor derelict in his constitutional obligations as set forth in the Charter of 1662. Nevertheless, the four members of the council led by Trumbull strode from the room in defense of their conviction that the Stamp Act was incompatible with Connecticut's traditional privilege of taxing itself.[3] Although he could not have known it then, as Jonathan Trumbull strode from the council chamber he was taking the first step along a route which would make him one of the most significant figures of the Revolutionary era.

The fact that Trumbull chose disobedience to London in 1765 was perhaps related to a number of factors. It might indeed have been true that the Lebanon merchant's dismal financial situation in the mid-1760s encouraged him to adopt a hostile position toward that nation whose merchants were making his own life so uncomfortable. Also, as a son of eastern Connecticut, he had very little choice but to repudiate the Stamp Act. The raging radicalism of eastern Connecticut would surely have been turned against Trumbull himself, had he followed a more moderate course during the crisis of 1765. Lebanon's leading citizen would have promptly found himself without a political base and thus without any hope of continued public recognition.[4] Yet, although one cannot completely dismiss Trumbull's financial situation or his political interest as motivating factors in his thinking in 1765, the evidence indicates that his response to the Stamp Act was dictated essentially by his fundamental Puritan orientation.

Despite his years at Harvard, as well as his immersion in the sophisticated worlds of business and politics, Trumbull, in his mature years, still functioned intellectually on the basis of that Puritan framework which had so colored the development of early Connecticut. In the face of the growing secularization of both American and Connecticut society,[5] Trumbull retained the conviction that Connecticut could fulfill its destiny only by continued attention to its mission as a Puritan Zion. To hold such a view meant inevitably that Trumbull would regard the mother country in much the way that it had been viewed by those of Hooker's generation. England, in short, was a cancer whose only significant characteristic was its unwillingness to adopt the truly Christian orientation which constituted the basis of Puritan Congregationalism. While a man of Trumbull's mentality might have been grateful for the sanity which England revealed in the Glorious Revolution by repudiating both popery and arbitrary government, evidence indicated that eighteenth-century Britain had come to be characterized by "extravagance, luxury, idleness, drunkenness, poverty, and crime."[6] British government had come to be corrupted by the frenetic race for position that dominated the thinking of the Whig magnates, and the nation's social order had fallen prey to the preoccupation with opulence which was reflected in the life-styles of the leadership of the era. As reports of the degradation and corruption of the mother country filtered across the Atlantic,[7] it is not surprising that a man such as Trumbull would have been unwilling to accept a more assertive British imperial policy in the 1760s.

Legislation such as the Sugar Act and the Stamp Act were but attempts by Britain's leaders to place on the shoulders of American manhood the yoke of burdensome taxation that had been long-borne by Britain's masses.[8] The people of eastern Connecticut were convinced that the revenue produced by these measures would be used to feed the luxurious tastes of the swarms of placehoulders and pensioners who cluttered the rolls of British military and civil lists.[9] Before long, America would be inundated by British placemen who would transfer their rapacious inclinations among the virtuous American populace.[10] No wonder, then, that Trumbull viewed the Stamp Act as but the first step in what ultimately would be the corruption and demoralization of pristine American society. Representing the freemen of Lebanon who had met to discuss the Stamp Act, Trumbull, in August, 1765, wrote to Governor Fitch:

> The People in this part of the Colony, are very Jealous for their Liberties; and Desire That The most Vigorous Exertions be made for the Repeal of the Late Act of Parliament, for Granting and Applying Certain Stamp Duties & Other Duties in the British Colonies . . . which they look on to be utterly subsersive of their Rights and Priviledges both by Charter, and as English Men. . . ."

As the Anglo-American controversy deepened in the late 1760s, Trumbull came more and more to believe that the British legislative innovations grew out of an insidious British plot to alter what constituted the natural, or pre-1763, relationship between the mother country and the colonies. Trumbull viewed the relationship as one in which the colonies owed allegiance only as long as Britain met her obligation of respecting those American liberties inherent in the colonial charters. Writing to William Samuel Johnson in London in 1767, Trumbull noted:

> Great Britain and her Colonies' interests' are mutual and inseparable; so long as the Colonies want protection and supplies of necessary manufactures from the mother country, it can't be their interest to separate, and it is always to the interest of the Mother country to Keep them dependent and employed in such productions. . . . But if violence or methods tending to violence be taken to maintain their dependence, it tends to hasten a separation. . . .[12]

Convinced that difficulties were thus the responsibility of the mother country, Trumbull concluded by 1768 that any unfortunate repercussions of the imperial controversy had their origins in London alone:

> The Inhabitants of the Colonies and Especially Ours are as loyal & Faithful subjects as perhaps any in his Majesty's Dominions, and have very little disposition to wrangle & finding fault with Government. The Matter of Duties for raising a Revenue, occasions of Unhappy dispute, which had better never have been moved—surely Our Interests are Mutual & Inseparable, & whatever tends to raise Jealousies, & create Alienations of Affections must prove hurtfull & injurious to both Countries if continued. I fear many hope to promote their private Interest by misrepresentation, & moving Strife & contentions.[13]

Although Trumbull had no doubts about his support of the Patriot position during the Stamp Act crisis, he did not serve as a spearhead of public opinion in Connecticut. Remaining true to the Trumbull *modus operandi* of never endangering one's public position, he rather allowed himself to be carried along to political prominence by the force of the radical pressure of the counties of eastern Connecticut. That he was in fact acceptable to the radicals was, of course, not unrelated to his known support of American resistance to British assertiveness.

But, Trumbull had two additional qualifications which were necessary for a man to be supported by eastern Connecticut. Firstly, he had kept on good terms with the "New Light" religious elements in the area. Despite his authorship of the 1743 bill which restricted itinerant preaching, he had managed by his judicious mediation in "New Light"-"Old Light" disputes in the 1740s and 1750s to convince the evangelicals that he was not essentially hostile.[14] Secondly, and of prime significance, Trumbull had quietly but definitely associated himself with the eastern Connecticut economic panacea of the period—the Susquehannah Company. Before he assumed the governorship in 1769, Trumbull did not speak out in support of the company which was formed in near-by Windham, but the evidence indicates that as early as 1761 the Lebanon merchant was a significant shareholder of the Susquehannah Company.[15] In every significant respect, then, Jonathan Trumbull was acceptable to the politically-maturing counties of eastern Connecticut. As a result, as eastern Connecticut roared to political supremacy in the election of 1766, Trumbull was swept along to the heights of public recognition.

In the months which led up to the election of 1766, the "Sons of Liberty" conducted an untiring and vicious campaign to defeat Governor Fitch. The "easterners" expanded their organization throughout eastern Connecticut's towns and even penetrated the area west of the river. Exploiting the hard times which all Connecticut had been facing since the end of the French and Indian War, the "Sons of Liberty" raged over and over that if Connecticut were to support leaders such as Fitch, the colony would not only lose its liberties, but suffer economic devastation as well. Too, the "Sons" introduced into partyless Connecticut a ticket of their own, supporting William Pitkin of Hartford, a leading merchant and friend to "liberty," for governor and Jonathan Trumbull for deputy-governor. Even though the fierce American opposition had moved the British Parliament to repeal the Stamp Act in February, 1766, the "easterners" kept up their drumbeat of campaigning, always declaring that Connecticut would have to possess leadership willing to oppose any future British tyranny. The campaign paid off handsomely. Sweeping the eastern towns and picking up some support among the economically-depressed element in western Connecticut, the Pitkin-Trumbull slate carried the day.

With eastern Connecticut in power following the election of 1766 and Trumbull in office as deputy-governor from 1766-1769 and as governor in 1769 following the death of William Pitkin, the Lebanon merchant must have felt secure that he was riding the wave of Connecticut's political future. For from the late 1760s to the outbreak of figthing at Lexington and Concord in April, 1755, Trumbull emerged as an energetic spoksman of eastern Connecticut's radical Patriot position. Indeed, Trumbull in these years left no doubt that under his leadership Connecticut would hesitate not a moment to protect and defend her traditional autonomy.

The imposition of the Townshend Duties in 1767, for example, evoked a predictable reaction from Deputy-Governor Trumbull. Writing to William Samuel Johnson, one of Connecticut's agents in London, Trumbull asserted that while the British should be assured that the American colonies did not seek a disruption of the Anglo-American relationship, they would not sit by peacefully while their liberties were abused.[16] Reflecting one of his basic fears—the corruption of American government—Trumbull was irked by the probable, use of the revenue which the British would derive from the new legislation:

> Support of Tax gatherers and Their Numerous Train, for rendering Governors and Judges independent of the people for their Support, and for the Maintenance of Troops in the Colonies, to Overawe them to Compliance with things grievous and hard to be born. . . .[17]

During the relatively calm period in Anglo-American relations between the repeal of the Townshend legislation and the final upheaval which stemmed from the Boston Tea Party of December 16, 1773, Jonathan Trumbull, now governor of the colony,[18] continued to reflect the philosophy and concerns of the eastern Connecticut radical Patriots.

One of the major concerns of eastern Connecticut in the early 1770s was the growing strength of the colony's Anglican parishes. From the early 1740s, Anglicanism had been a beneficiary of the swirling controversy among the "New Lights" and "Old Lights" among Connecticut's Congregationalists. Offering a haven of order and conservatism, the Anglican Church had managed to swell itself from seven clergy and a dozen or so parishes in 1740 to fourteen rectors and 30 churches in 1760.[19] While Connecticut's Puritans hardly relished the growth of the Anglican Church at any time or under any circumstances, there were two reasons for an increase in concern in the pre-Revolutionary period.

It had become clear in the crisis over the Stamp Act, first of all, that Connecticut's Anglicans were almost uniformly in support of the mother country.[20] Rejecting completely the charter and natural right justifications for resistance to British legislation, the Anglicans focused upon the necessity of loyalty to the empire. Even worse, from the point of view of the colony's radicals, the Anglicans saw the entire colonial position as but a facade behind which "cunning" politicos served their own inclinations for advancement.[21] Already infuriated by the political softness of the Anglicans, the eastern Connecticut leaders were then terrified to learn of the possibility that an Anglican Episcopate would be established in the American colonies. It became widely known throughout the colony that Connecticut's Churchmen in the late 1760s and 1770s were appealing to London that the loyalty of the colony's faithful could most appropriately be rewarded by the appointment of an American bishop.[22]

The prospect of an Anglican Episcopate evoked an immediate reaction from Governor Trumbull. Arbitrary taxes and unbearable imperial supervision had been enough to convince Trumbull of the corrupt design of London; an Anglican bishop in Connecticut was no less than absolute proof that Britain truly represented the devil's hosts in seeking to demoralize the colony. He wrote in December, 1769, to William Samuel Johnson in London, asserting that the creation of an Anglican Episcopate in Connecticut would not only put the Congregational Establishment in danger but would ultimately provide the British with an ecclesiastical base from which they could strengthen their secular power.[23] Johnson, a communicant of the Anglican Church, sought to soothe Trumbull by answering that an Anglican bishop would have influence only over those who voluntarily accepted his theological and ecclesiastical authority.[24] Such a response, obviously, would not satisfy the puritan Trumbull, and Johnson wrote shortly afterwards that he would certainly oppose the appointment of an Anglican bishop, since that was the position clearly reflected by public opinion in Connecticut. While the debate over an American Episcopate was ultimately cut short by the Revolutionary War, Jonathan Trumbull stridently maintained his anti-Anglican posture in the pre-war years, thus perfectly reflecting the viewpoint of his eastern-Connecticut political base.

Perhaps an even more decisive indicaton of the rapport that existed in the pre-Revolutionary years between Trumbull and eastern Connecticut was the governor's increasingly assertive position regarding the aspirations of the Susquehannah Company. The promoters of the company generally had not enjoyed much success in the 1760s. In 1763, the King in Council had decreed that the proposed settlement in Pennsylvania not take place, and throughout the rest of the decade the company did not have sufficient strength in the General Assembly to have its expansionist plan adopted by the colony.[25] By the early 1770s, however, factors effected a change in the company's prospects.

First of all, in the pre-Revolutionary years, Connecticut farmers realized that much of the colony's settled land was fast losing its fertility. Constant cultivation and primitive agricultural methods had combined to exhaust considerable portions of Connecticut's farmlands. While much Connecticut land was still both arable and uncultivated, small farmers found that such land was in the hands of absentee landlords, who, speculating on probable future profits, would only rent their property.[26] The small farmer's plight was further complicated by a rapid increase in population in the decade and a half before the Revolution. Based essentially on an extremely high birth rate, Connecticut's population increased by more than 50,000 between 1762 and 1774, making the colony the second most densely populated colony in New England.[27] The combination of paucity of arable land for sale and the population increase naturally resulted in rampant land hunger among Connecticut's small farmers. Under these circumstances, the plans of the Susquehannah Company began to appear to many residents of the colony as the most likely solution to the problems of the small farmer. Thus, by the early 1770s, the proposal of the Susquehannah Company that the General Assembly support its claim in Pennsylvania was gaining favor in the colony. In May, 1771, the General Assembly, therefore, voted that the Colony of Connecticut would assume as its own the Susquehannah Company claim.[28] The legislature asserted that the territory was clearly within the boundaries of the colony's charter and set up a committee to collect evidence of the legality of the claim.[29]

While the support received in the General Assembly was clearly to the advantage of the Susquehannah Company, the governorship of Jonathan Trumbull was another major factor in improving its fortunes. By 1773, the Connecticut claim to Pennsylvania land was still languishing in London, and the members of the company grew restless. Trumbull, long a member of the company, and obviously aware of the general support the Susquehannah scheme had in eastern Connecticut, promptly responded to the company's request for action. Trumbull went before the October, 1773, session of the General Assembly and delivered a ringing expansionist speech. The governor declared that since the power of Connecticut could only be enhanced by the territory in Pennsylvania, and, since the colony's claim was clearly sound, Connecticut should hasten to establish its authority over the area in question.[30] Encouraged by Trumbull, the pro-Susquehannah Assembly responded. By January, 1774, the Connecticut General Assembly had extended its jurisdiction over the Susquehannah claim in the Wyoming Valley of Pennsylvania by organizing the area into the township of Westmoreland.[31] The Assembly also created a committee to advance the colony's claim in London and then ordered the cooperative Governor Trumbull to issue a proclamation prohibiting any settlement in Westmoreland without its permission.[32] Although this Connecticut thrust into Pennsylvania was to be soon interrupted by the Revolution,

Jonathan Trumbull, as a true son and political dependent of eastern Connecticut, had done all within his power for the Susquehannah cause.

While Trumbull was an earnest advocate of the interests of eastern Connecticut regarding both the Anglican and Susquehannah issues, the true significance of his governorship was his unqualified support of the Patriot position as the imperial controversy exploded in 1774. Through the wracking debate which the news of the Coercive Acts brought to Connecticut, Jonathan Trumbull, responding on the basis of his provincial, Puritan outlook, proved to be a staunch supporter of eastern Connecticut's radical posture.

While Connecticut's radicals had been busy throughout 1773 demanding a boycott on the tea that Parliament had permitted the East India Company to ship to America, it was the news of the Coercive Acts of 1774 which served as the spark to the colony's revolutionary fuse.[33] Maintaining that if the good people of the Bay Colony were allowed to be crushed under the weight of British tyranny, then all of America would soon be equally enslaved, the radicals of eastern Connecticut inundated the colony with fiery appeals. The yeomen of Connecticut were asked by one unsigned appeal to

> Conceive of a Land Tax grappled upon your Estates, and imagine your Wheat, your Beef, your Pork, your Butter and Cheese, and your Teams, all tax'd to maintain Pensioners and Placemen, and support the Extravagancies of a Bankrupt Nation . . . The Bishops they say are linked in this diabolical scheme, and it is not possible they soon will take Tythes of all our Children. . .?[34]

Radicals, ignoring established political units, called special town meetings throughout eastern Connecticut to denounce British tyranny and pledge support for Boston.[35]

Emboldened by their political strength and undoubtedly convinced that their cherished charter rights were at stake, the colony's radicals embarked upon no less than a purge of Connecticut's moderates and conservatives. Those who spoke out against the defense of American rights by such "wild and childish licentious" acts as the Boston Tea Party promptly felt the strength of the radicals. Eastern Connecticut communities such as Windham, Preston, Pomfret, Mansfield, and Ashford acted in town meetings either to silence or expel those "Tories" who did not hold "Sentiments more kind to their Countrymen."[36] Those who did not take the admonitions of the radicals with sufficient seriousness soon received treatment that made the Ingersoll affair of Stamp Act days look benign. One Francis Green, a Bostonian who had pledged his loyalty to Governor Hutchinson, made the almost fatal error of visiting radical Windham. Early one July, 1774, morning, the local patriots hauled a cannon to the door of the tavern where Green had been staying and made it clear that unless the visitor promptly removed himself, the inn would be immediately subject to architectural restructuring. Green, acutely putting his safety before his honor, quit Windham with dispatch.[37]

Although it was certainly no consolation to him, Green was certainly not the only conservative to feel the radical force. A comparable confrontation with extra-legal pressure was experienced in the town of Hebron by the Tory, Anglican priest, the Reverend Samuel Peters. Peters had distinguished himself during the summer of 1774 by his unrestrained denunciation of the radical tide. To Peters, the entire radical surge was nothing more than a blatant attempt to use the imperial issue as a device by which cunning men could continue their control of the colony.[38] By August, 1774, the local radicals had obviously become weary of the Tory's scathing remarks. Peters found himself and his home searched by a delegation of the Sons of Liberty. The following month he received even more attention when he was forced by a mob of over 300 to recant his political views on the Hebron Green. The vicious nature of the mob convinced Peters that neither his person nor property were safe, and he shorty afterward sought the protection of the British troops in Boston.[39] The circumstances of the cleric's departure from Hebron help to explain why Peters spent so much of the rest of his life castigating the "drunken barbarous People" of Connecticut.[40]

While the radicals of eastern Connecticut raged during the summer and fall of 1774, the value of a Whig governor became quite apparent, for, as Clifford K. Shipton has so well put it, "Trumbull believed that a man's right to protection by the state was qualified by his political opinions."[41] Trumbull's correspondence does contain references to his anxiety over the activities of extra-legal groups, but the fact remains that while the Connecticut Whigs were physically enforcing their politcal philosophy, Trumbull did not lift a finger to protect the assaulted Tories.[42] Indeed, when Governor Gage requested that Trumbull punish the members of the mob active in the intimidation of the Boston Green, Trumbull replied with the evasion that "full provision is made by law for such offences."[43] To Samuel Peters' plea for assistance against the Hebron Sons of Liberty, Trumbull was even more blunt, maintaining that such protection "was not in his power, the people had assumed their natural right to judge for themselves, and to punish Jacobites."[44]

Trumbull continued to reveal that he was the perfect man to preside as the Whig tide carried Connecticut toward Revolution when, in 1775, Tories in Fairfield and Litchfield Counties joined together to assert their allegiance to the Crown. They asserted in conventions in January and February that the constitutional power of the British

Empire resided with "the King, Lords, and Commons." Repudiating the endless extra-legal Whig conventions, associations, committees and mobs which had determined so much of Connecticut policy in the last decade, the moderates argued that there was no need for any "other political Guides or Guardians than the Assembly and Officers Constitutionally appointed by them to keep the Peace and order of the Colony."[45] A clearer challenge to the Whigs could not have been presented—a fact not unrecognized by the radicals.

The hapless Tories found Trumbull less than sympathetic to their objectives to Patriot measures. Governor Trumbull went before the March, 1775, session of the General Assembly to malign the Tories as "depraved, malignant, avaricious, and haughty," and called for "manly action against those who by Force and Violence seek your ruin and Destruction."[46] The Whig-dominated Assembly heeded the governors' call and passed legislation providing for an investigation of militia officers suspected of Toryism and then enacted a bill to establish a committee to examine suspected loyalists in Tory communities such as Newtown and Ridgefield.[47]

While Connecticut Whig and Tory were moving closer toward collision, April, 1775, brought the news of the outbreak of hostilities at Lexington and Concord. As both moderate and radical reacted with fear and fervor, it was to both that the period of contention was to be replaced by one in which the sword was to be the decisive instrument. Typical of the reaction of the Connecticut Patriots was that of Jonathan Trumbull. The governor, upon hearing of the bloodshed in Massachusetts, hesitated not a moment before opening the family store in Lebanon and personally supplying the troops of the local militia regiment who were itching to march to Cambridge.[48] Trumbull, as he had since the Stamp Act crisis of 1765, determined that his course was to be resistance to what he regarded as the brutal British attempt to destroy the traditional liberties of the American colonies. That Trumbull approached the imperial question with such instinctual certainly might not have spoken much of his political sophistication; yet, it was well for the cause of American independence that he did, for Jonathan Trumbull would need every ounce of determination at his disposal as he bore the crushing burdens of the Connecticut governorship during the desperate years of the Revolutionary War.

War Governor: Continental Affairs

I т would have been difficult, indeed, to predict in 1775 that Jonathan Trumbull of Connecticut would emerge during the Revolutionary War as one of the major contributors to the American victory. As a merchant, Trumbull had revealed an almost inexorable predilection for failure. Although he had enjoyed the comfortable life-style of a prosperous merchant-prince for over 30 years, he had been saved from bankruptcy and its accompanying humiliations only by the Anglo-American rift of the 1760s and 1770s. During his years of financial embarrassment, further, Trumbull's conduct with his creditors did little honor to his name or reputation. As a public figure, Trumbull's careful and prudent behavior had enabled him to become a principal beneficiary of Connecticut's sectional conflict. As a result, he had been carried to the offices of deputy-governor and governor on the basis largely of eastern Connecticut's sudden rise to political power after the Stamp Act crisis. Such credentials, in short, would hardly have indicated the magnificence of the contribution Trumbull was to make to Connecticut and to the nation during the demanding years of the Revolutionary War.

Indeed, that contribution is perhaps even more impressive in light of the succession of personal tragedies which Jonathan Trumbull experienced during the war years. His first loss was that of his first-born daughter, Faith Trumbull. Born in 1743, Faith had been educated by Master Tisdale in Lebanon and then had been sent to Boston to complete her studies.[1] Faith must have been an attractive young lady, for she was able to reinforce the family's social position by becoming the bride of Jedediah Huntington of Norwich, one of eastern Connecticut's most eligible bachelors.[2] The social and political prominence of the Huntington family was based upon the accomplishments of Jedediah's father, Jabez. The elder Huntington was a Yale graduate (1741) who made a fortune in the West India trade and went on to become a major political figure in Connecticut.[3] The family's social position was reflected in Jedediah being ranked second in his Harvard class of 1763.[4] He then assisted his father in the family business until he devoted more and more of his time to political matters, becoming one of the most staunch eastern Connecticut Whigs by the late 1760s and early 1770s.[5] Jedediah Huntington developed into a first-class officer during the Revolutionary War and put together an impressive record of service.[6] Faith Trumbull Huntington, however, was not to live to share the honors accorded her husband.

The Trumbull Family correspondence indicates that Faith was ill in 1775. Governor Trumbull wrote to his son Joseph, the commissary-general of the American Army, in October, 1775, to request that Huntington, a colonel of the 20th Regiment of Connecticut Militia, try to be relieved for a few days of his duties with Washington's army outside Boston so that he could visit Faith.[7] It appears that Huntington did make it home so see the ill Faith, as she died on Nevember 24, 1775.[8] The circumstances of the illness and death of Faith are difficult to understand, since the only information available is the following excerpt from the autobiography of John Trumbull:

> About noon of that day [June 17, 1775, the day of the Battle of Bunker Hill] I had a momentary interview with my favorite sister, the wife of Colonel Huntington. . . . The novelty of military scenes excited great curiosity throughout the country, and my sister was one of a party of young friends who were attracted to visit the Army before Boston. She was a woman of deep and affectionate sensibility, and the moment of her visit was most unfortunate. She found herself surrounded, not by 'the pomp and circumstances of glorious war,' but in the midst of all its horrible realities. She saw too clearly the life of danger and hardship upon which her husband . . . entered, and it overcame her strong, but too sensitive mind. She became deranged, and died the following November. . . .[9]

One can conclude that Faith must have been a person susceptible to emotional distress who suffered a severe psychological trauma while viewing the carnage of battle. The experience perhaps so disturbed her that she experienced a state of depression which culminated in her suicide.[10]

The tragic death of Faith was but the first of the family's afflictions during the war years. Before Jonathan Trumbull could have adjusted to the loss of his daughter, he was faced with the illness and death of his son Joseph. The eldest Trumbull son had enjoyed substantial public recognition in the 1760s and 1770s. He had served in the Connecticut General Assembly (1767-1773), been a member of the colony's Committee of Correspondence (1773), and was chosen to represent Connecticut as an alternate delegate at the First Continental Congress (1774).[11] On the basis of his mercantile experience and his public record, he was appointed by the Assembly in April, 1775, to serve as the commissary-general of the Connecticut troops assembled near Boston.[12] He proved to be so successful in this capacity that, with Washington's urging, the Continental Congress appointed him commissary-general of the American Army on July 19, 1775.[13] Although Joseph Trumbull's efforts as commissary-general were not unrecognized,[14] the task was fraught with endless difficulties. Transportation was laborious and uncertain; purchasing was impeded by a constant shortage of funds, state embargoes, and wildly-fluctuating currency values; and agents of the continental commissariat often found themselves in competition for provisions with state agents.[15] Along with the constant complications occasioned by these difficulties, Joseph Trumbull experienced a particularly bitter clash with General Schuyler in 1776 regarding the prerogative of the commissary-general in supplying the northern army.[16]

While Joseph Trumbull's position in the controversy was ultimately supported by both Washington and Congress, he decided to resign his position in the spring of 1777 when Congress put into effect a scheme for the reorganization of the commissariat which he felt to be unworkable.[17] Yet, Joseph Trumbull's resignation as commissary-general did not signify any unwillingness to continue to shoulder public responsibilities, for in November, 1777, he accepted an appointment to the Board of War.[18] He was, however, to continue no longer in the public service. His tenure as commissary-general had so shattered his health that when he was stricken with a cold in the winter of 1777-1778, he underwent a physical decline from which he was not to recover. By February, 1778, he had experienced paralysis of his left side and was suffering from jaundice.[19] Although he appeared to be recovering during the summer from his afflictions, Joseph Trumbull had a relapse and died on July 23, 1778.[20]

A final personal loss which Jonathan Trumbull had to bear during the war was the death of his wife, Faith Trumbull. By the late 1770s, in her sixties, Faith Robinson Trumbull began to suffer from a dropsical affliction which finally took her life on May 29, 1780.[21] She had been an affectionate wife and mother, and one who understood and bound herself to the nation's cause for which her husband and sons were laboring. During the Revolutionary War she was a tireless worker on behalf of Connecticut troops and their families. She supported charities, instituted clothing drives, and encouraged soldiers' wives to bear the burdens of loneliness and economic privation.[22] It was said that during one of the clothing drives that took place during the war, Faith Trumbull rose to the occasion by contributing to the cause "a magnificent scarlet cloak" which had been given to her by Count Rochambeau.[23] The death of Faith Robinson Trumbull, then, deprived Trumbull of a loving and philosophically compatible mate.[24]

No one, of course, can measure the impact of these personal circumstances upon Jonathan Trumbull. Yet, it would appear that the emotional cost to Trumbull of these deaths was high. Although he was a man who rarely functioned on an emotional basis, he demonstrated throughout his life a deep attachment to his wife and chldren. His correspondence with his sons during the war reveals a man who was not too immersed in public concerns to forget the family ties of affection and concern.[25]

Perhaps most indicative of Trumbull's tender regard for his family was his attitude toward the artistic inclination of his youngest son.

Toward the conclusion of the war,[26] John Trumbull decided to devote himself completely to his development as a painter. The scene at the Trumbull home in Lebanon when John announced his intention to go abroad and study under Benjamin West has often been described.[27] Governor Trumbull labored manfully to convince his son that a career in the law would prove to be far more productive than labors with the "pencil." Finally, when his arguments were clearly running short, he closed with the ringing assertion that "Connecticut is not Athens." Students of Trumbull have concluded that his unwillingness to see John go to London to study art was based upon his provincial, Puritan approach to the question of a vocational choice. While there was perhaps something of this in Trumbull's position, his correspondence with John while the young artist was studying with West reveals that the more important element in Trumbull's attitude was his desire not to be separated from his youngest son. All through 1783, 1784, and 1785, Trumbull wrote letter after letter to John congratulating him on the progress he seemed to have been making in his studies, but making clear that he wanted the young man by his side in Lebanon. In November, 1784, he wrote: "I am overjoyed to know your pictures have so much merit as to begin to be productive. I wish your study . . . may admit your return sooner than you have hitherto mentioned."[28] As John seemed impervious to the father's plea, the retired governor become pathetically blunt by 1785. He wrote to John in April noting that the harsh winter had been difficult for him, obviously implying that shortness of time left to him made it imperative that the son return.[29] The old man, tired and lonely and growing ill, was at last showing the strain of his labors and his personal losses.[30]

Yet, Trumbull's loneliness and illness were not apparent until he had retired from public office. During the war years, when the fate of his state and nation were being determined, Jonathan Trumbull proved himself to be one of the pillars upon which the rising American nation was constructed. Not to be seen was the confused merchant who held off creditors with questionable devices, the opportunistic politician who very carefully looked before he even contemplated leaping, nor even the affectionate husband and father who was wracked by one bitter family loss after another. Rather, one could have seen only a strong, competent statesman who bore successfully the burdens of wartime administrations, and, who, in the process, came to be viewed by his contemporaries as one of the most potent instruments in the achievement of American independence.

From the time when the alarm of Lexington and Concord swept through New England until the nation rejoiced in 1783 over the conclusion of the Treaty of Paris, Jonathan Trumbull was at the center of the American war effort. He almost alone bore the responsibility of the mobilization of Connecticut's physical and economic resources. Seeing his state constantly menaced by the British regulars who occupied New York for the better part of the war, he nevertheless concentrated completely on the more crucial matter of contributing to the maintenance of Washington's army. Shipment upon shipment of vital supplies went to the Continental Army while town officials througout Connecticut were demanding that the security of their homes required higher priority than Continental supply. And, as the war years brought the inevitable reaction against taxes, economic controls, and the draft, it was Trumbull who by word and example encouraged the sunshine patriots to gird themselves for a continuation of the sacrifices necessary for the vindication of the nation's cause. Finally, when the end of the war brought fear in Connecticut that an expansion of the powers of Congress would diminish the state's historic autonomy, it was the aging Trumbull who put his declining political reputation to its last test by demanding that Connecticut support Congress in its realistic attempt to tighten the bonds of union by the creation of a strong central goverment.

The fact that Jonathan Trumbull assumed such a strongly nationalistic position during the Revolutionary War was related to his Puritan-oriented political outlook. Throughout the war years, Trumbull associated the cause of American nationhood with that of the realization of God's plan for the salvation of mankind. In June, 1776, Trumbull interpreted the struggle to the freemen of Connecticut in obviously Lockean terms:

> The Race of Mankind was made in a State of Innocence and Freedom, subjected only to the laws of God. . . . But through Pride and Ambition, the Kings and Princes of the World, appointed by the People the Guardians of their Lives and Liberties . . . degenerated into Tyrants. . . . An unnatural King has risen up—violated his sacred Obligations, and by the Advice of evil Counsellors, attempted to wrest from us, their Children, the sacred Rights we justly claim, and which have been ratified and established by solemn compact with, and ratified by, his Predecessors.[31]

And in calling out the Connecticut militia for service in New York some two months later, his proclamation had the ring of an Old Testament quotation:

> . . . Be roused therefore and alarmed to stand forth in our just and glorious cause. Join yourselves to . . . the companies of militia now ordered to New York. . . . Stand forth for our defence. Play the man for God, and for the cities of our God. May the Hosts, the God of the armies of Israel, be your Captain, your Leader, your Conductor and Saviour.[32]

To the Puritan Trumbull there could, of course, be no compromise with the forces of evil. The British came to represent unadulterated darkness and corruption. Describing their conduct before the evacuation of Boston, he said: "Burning and destroying our towns, robbing our property, trampling on . . . places dedicated to divine worship and service, and cruel treatment of the persons so unhappy as to fall into their hands, are injuries of the first magnitude. Every subtle art, as well as arms, are used against us."[33]

But if Trumbull believed that the enemy represented evil, he was just as certain that the ultimate design of God was the victory of American arms. Writing to the Connecticut delegates in Congress in July, 1775, he advised them "to have your eyes upon the supreme director of Events for protection and Defence. He is good, He is a stronghold in the day of Trouble, He goes with them that put their Trust in him."[34] After Washington's defeat in the Battle of Long Island in August, 1776, when gloom and hopelessness characterized the American cause, Trumbull never doubted that the Lord would rescue America. In a proclamation issued in September, 1776, he encouraged his fellow citizens "to supplicate for his Mercy, for Wisdom and Direction . . . so the free and the independent States may be radicated, confirmed, established, built up, and caused to flourish, and to become a Praise in the whole earth."[35]

Trumbull's faith was undoubtedly that which was his most significant strength during the trials of the war. It enabled him to overcome defeat and despair during the period between Lexington and Saratoga when British arms succeeded in besting Washington's troops. Perhaps more importantly, Trumbull's faith encouraged him to view the struggle from a national, indeed a cosmological viewpoint, so that he was never tempted to lapse into that localism and provincialism which was probably America's greatest weakness during the Revolutionary War. Finally, it was Trumbull's faith that he was doing the Lord's work which enabled him to continue to bear his public responsibilities in the face of family tragedy.

And yet, Trumbull's contribution to the war effort was made possible by more than just his nationalistic view of the struggle or his faith in the rightness of the American cause. Trumbull, first of all, was well served during the Revolutionary War by the experience in military supply and transportation he had acquired during the intercolonial wars. Too, Trumbull's contribution was also made possible by the relative political stability which Connecticut enjoyed during the war. Connecticut, as an essentially autonomous colony in 1775, did not have to go through a difficult period of political reorganization as did most of the states during the early years of the war. Finally, it must be noted that Trumbull was aided during the war by the essentially Whig consensus that existed in Connecticut. Although Tory sentiment had been strong in the western towns before the war, the outbreak of hostilities, as well as action undertaken by Governor Trumbull and the General Assembly, served to silence or drive from the state those with Loyalist inclinations. As a result, Connecticut was spared the internal Whig-Tory hostilities that weakened the war effort of other states, particularly those in the South.

Thus, from the outset of hostilities, Jonathan Trumbull was inclined and was able to make a substantive contribution to Patriot success. Through the rooms of the Trumbull house in Lebanon passed a number of the most significant figures of the Revolutionary era: Washington, Knox, Sullivan, Putnam, Franklin, Samuel Adams, John Adams, Jay, Jefferson, Rochambeau, Tiernay, Lafayette, Lauzun, and Chastellux.[36] The adjoining building, formerly used as a mercantile depot, came to be known as the "War Office," the site where Trumbull met with his Council of Safety some 900 times between 1775 and 1783,[37] and where Trumbull organized the Connecticut war effort. Swift riders on Narragansett pacers brought Trumbull war news from every theater of operations, and Trumbull in turn mobilized the resources of the state to meet the endless requests of Washington and his subordinates for troops and supplies.

It was, of course, in the field of logistics that Trumbull played such a crucial role during the Revolutionary War. That Trumbull was able to do so was related to a number of factors. Connecticut was fortunate in possessing especially productive river valleys such as the Connecticut, the Housatonic, and the Thames. These regions brought forth large crops of corn, rye, wheat, oats, barley, flax, hemp, vegetables, and fruit. While the heavily-forested lands of the northeast and northwest sections of the state were always grain-importing areas, the woodlands were worked for lumber, pitch, potash, and maple sugar, while the hillsides were excellent grazing areas for cattle, horses, mules, and sheep. Connecticut's productivity proved to be especially helpful for the war effort, since the state never experienced the destruction and razing which always came with enemy occupation. Except for a few raids on Connecticut's coastal towns, the state was able throughout the war to conduct its agricultural enterprises without interference from the enemy.

Yet, Trumbull's efforts to make Connecticut the "Provisions State" during the war required more than the Governor's patriotism, the land's productivity, and the lack of sustained British military pressure. Trumbull and the General Assembly, acting generally in concert, were responsible for legislation which contributed greatly to Connecticut's logistical efforts during the Revolutionary War.

First of all, Connecticut made a sustained attempt to stave off that uncontrolled inflation which in so many states made agricultural producers unwilling to sell to state or Continental Commissary agents.[38] Connecticut, like most states, quickly jumped on the expedient of issuing paper money as a means of meeting the expenses of the war. In April, 1775, the General Assembly ordered the emission of £50,000.[39] The very next month, another £50,000 was issued.[40] The state continued on its paper money ways until by 1783 the General Assembly had provided for the emission of £1,200,000 in such notes.[41] Yet, the state was relatively responsible in its utilization of paper money, especially when one notes that some six states exceeded the figure of Connecticut, with Massachusetts, for example, issuing over £13,000,000 during the course of the war.[42] While it is not possible to state that it was the influence of Trumbull that kept Connecticut's emissions of paper money at a reasonable level, it is likely that his views on the matter were not insignificant. Throughout the war, Trumbull was "a bullionist pure and simple" who decried both the state and the Continental attempts to underwrite the war expenditures on any other basis but that of "pay as you go."[43]

Along with his anti-paper money position, Trumbull favored increased wartime taxation as a means to control inflation.[44] While the specific influence of Trumbull's views on the actions of the General Assembly is again difficult to discern, the Connecticut legislators did respond during the war to the highly unpopular but necessary step of imposing greater taxes.[45] Early in 1776, the General Assembly voted a tax of four pence on the pound and ordered it collected before June, 1777.[46] Later in the same year, the Assembly established three additional taxes, all of which were payable before the end of 1777.[47] Although the Assembly was forced to alter its taxation policy somewhat during the war to answer the protests of agrarians who bitterly denounced both the increased rates and real property basis on which they were levied,[48] taxes were kept high throughout the war as a means of meeting the state's expenses and curbing the inflationary thrust.

More important, perhaps, than the anti-inflationary actions of Trumbull and the Assembly in contributing to Connecticut's logistical potential were measures taken to cut the exportation of the state's produce and manufactures. In 1775, Trumbull sought from the General Assembly an embargo upon foodstuffs, products of the West Indies, and various materials, such as gunpowder, which were specifically needed for the military.[49] The Assembly responded throughout the war with a series of fairly comprehensive embargo measures.[50] Although the Connecticut embargo was responsible for scores of special applications for trade permits which Trumbull and his council had to wade through during the war, a furious altercation with Schuyler and the leading figures in New York,[51] and a clandestine trade between western Connecticut and Long Island which Trumbull was really never able to stop throughout the war, the embargo nevertheless was a major factor in making possible the logistical support which Connecticut provided to both state and Continental troops.

Connecticut's contribution to the supplying of American troops was related also to the outstanding commissary staff which worked under the direction of Governor Trumbull and the Council of Safety. Men such as Joseph Trumbull, Elijah Hubbard, and Jeremiah Wadsworth labored at various stages of the war to oversee the efforts of Connecticut's commissariat. Overcoming poor roads, exposure, uncertain pay, and bitter conflicts with Continental agents, the agents and teamsters of the state's commissariat proved equal to almost every demand that was made upon them during the Revolutionary War.

On the basis of these factors, then, Connecticut was able to function throughout the war at an extremely high level of logistical efficiency. At the beginning of the war, in May, 1775, the Connecticut General Assembly adopted a ration schedule for state troops that was later to serve as a model for the Continental Commissariat.[52] Each soldier was to be provided daily with three-quarters of a pound of pork or one pound of beef, one pound of flour, and three pints of beer. In addition, each man was to be supplied with "one jill of rum to each man upon fatigue per day," along with milk, molasses, soap, candles, vinegar, coffee, chocolate, sugar, tobacco, onions, and vegetables. Each week's ration would include as well a half a pint of rice or a pint of corn meal, six ounces of butter, and three pints of peas or beans.[53] Commissaries were to receive a commission of one and one-half percent upon all the supplies purchased, and throughout the war years the General Assembly gave commissaries and town selectmen comprehensive powers in purchasing or impressing provisions.[54]

The Connecticut system of supply was also exceptionally efficient in providing clothing for the state troops both in the militia and the Continental regiments. Generally speaking, the state handled this aspect of supply by establishing a quota for each town and then pressuring the local selectmen to make sure that their towns provided the requisite amounts.[55] The excellence of the state's efforts was demonstrated throughout the war, but it was especially apparent during Washington's terrible winter at Valley Forge in 1777-1778. At this time, more than two-thirds of Washington's troops were practically barefoot[56] and thousands went without blankets in the dead of winter.[57] The sight was such an extraordinarily tragic one that even the stoic commander wrote in anguish: "Our sick naked, our well naked, our unfortunate men in captivity naked!"[58] Yet, the leadership of Connecticut did not contribute to the breakdown in the supply of clothing that had taken place. In March, 1778, Washington acknowledged, rather, the superiority of Connecticut's performance in a letter to

Governor Trumbull: "Among the troops unfit for duty and returned for want of clothing, none of your State are included. The care of your legislature in providing clothing . . . for their men is highly laudable, and reflects the greatest honor upon their patriotism and humanity."[59]

Nevertheless, the recognition that Connecticut received during the Revolutionary War as the "Provisions State" was really not accorded on the basis of the state's everyday provisioning efforts of its own troops. Rather, Connecticut was recognized for its distinguished logistical effort in coming to the rescue of the American forces on three critical occasions. While there were many factors indeed which contributed to the ability of the American troops at Yorktown in October, 1781, to be in a position to sing "The World Turned Upside Down" while the troops of Cornwallis stacked their arms, not the least was the service which Connecticut had provided to the American cause at crucial stages in the war.

The winter of 1777-1778 has been called the "Gethsemane" of the American army.[60] It was the period when, although Saratoga had had a favorable impact upon the court of Louis XVI, the American Congress sat for months without hearing from its commissioners in Paris as to whether France had agreed to become an ally of the United States. It was the period when the so-called "Conway Cabal" was flourishing as members of Congress were disgruntled with Washington's showing at Brandywine and Germantown, and Howe's subsequent occupation of Philadelphia, the seat of Congress. And finally, it was the time when the American army was in the process of disintegrating. After starting the campaign of 1777 with almost 10,000 troops, Washington wound up wintering at Valley Forge with a bleeding army of 3,000.[61]

Washington, failed by a deteriorating commissariat and ignored by eastern Pennsylvania's farmers, was faced with the collapse of his army. Although disliking the expedient, he was forced to resort to a program of impressment to maintain his force. In late December, 1777, he issued a proclamation that farmers within 70 miles of Valley Forge had to thresh one-half of their grain by February and the other half by March. He then sent out foraging parties of troops to impress foodstuffs and teams for transport. The step, while successful in bringing substantial quanities of provisions to the American camp, in the long run probably hurt rather than aided Washington's cause. The troops, ordered to conduct themselves with patience in dealing with the neighborhood farmers, functioned with a ruthlessness and thoughtlessness that effected the alienation of eastern Pennsylvania. Washington's men used overt force in impressing provisions, and, perhaps expressing the frustration they must have felt at their plight, were responsible for useless destruction of property. Some bands of foraging parties were so foolish as to destroy the provisions and timber of iron forges in the area, thus rendering them inoperative.[62] Such activity naturally infuriated the local population and made the area an unlikely source of provisions for American troops. Clearly, then, the policy of impressment as it was carried out by Washington's troops was not to be the panacea to extricate the American army from its logistical nightmare, and thus by January, 1778, Washington had abandoned the practice.[63]

Through the bitter months of early 1778, Washington was provisioned and his army maintained by a number of expedients. Special arrangements were made through the Quartermaster Department to transport supplies from North Carolina, Virginia, and Maryland. Congress also appointed state purchasing commissioners for counties in the middle states who were largely successful because they were able to offer higher prices than had the agents of the commissariat. Finally, special appeals went out from Washington to state governors such as Clinton of New York, Livingston of New Jersey, Read of Delaware, Johnson of Maryland, Henry of Virginia, and Trumbull of Connecticut, requesting that they mobilize the resources of their state to meet Washington's crisis.[64] While each of these governors made a significant contribution to the maintenance of Washington's army, no contribution was more crucial than that of Jonathan Trumbull.

Washington wrote to Governor Trumbull on February 6, 1778:

> I must take the liberty of addressing you on a subject which, although out of your sphere, I am fully persuaded will have every possible attention in your power to give. It is the alarming situation of the army on account of provision. I shall not undertake minutely to investigate the causes of this, but there is the strongest reason to believe that its existence cannot be of long duration, unless more constant, regular, and larger supplies of meat kind are furnished. . . . I am assured that [the middle states] . . . are nearly exhausted in this instance . . . and as any relief that can be obtained from . . . southern States will be but partial . . . we must turn our views to the eastward. I must therefore, sir, entreat you in the most earnest terms, and by that zeal which has so eminently distinguished your character in the present arduous struggle, to give every countenance . . . to forward supplies of cattle. . . . I know your wishes to promote the service in every possible degree will render any apology unnecessary, and that the bare state of facts will be admitted as a full and ample justification for the trouble it is like to occasion you.[65]

Trumbull, as Washington knew he would, immediately began to organize Connecticut to meet the request.

Meeting with his Council of Safety, Trumbull delegated to one of the Connecticut commissaries, Colonel Henry Champion of Colchester, the task of collecting cattle to be driven to Valley Forge.[66] Champion set out from Lebanon to round up as many head as possible throughout eastern Connecticut. Aided by endless dispatches which Trumbull sent to farmers,[67] Champion was able to collect a herd of 300 at Hartford.[68] Then, Champion and his son Epaphroditus began the long trek to Valley Forge. Moving into New York, crossing the Hudson at King's Ferry, passing through upper Jersey and over the Delaware, the herd finally reached the famished troops west of the Schuykill.[69] That Washington's troops were in dire straits at the time is revealed by the fact that the entire herd was devoured within five days of its arrival. Epaphroditus Champion was said to have remarked that the beef had been eaten so thoroughly that "you might have made a knife out of every bone."[70]

Through the winter and spring of 1778, herd after herd of Connecticut cattle were driven to Valley Forge under the direction of Trumbull and Champion.[71] These provisions, along with emergency shipments from New York, New Jersey, Maryland, and Virginia, were the crucial element in maintaining the American army through spring when the reorganization of the commissariat was able to bring forth regular provisioning of Washington's troops.

The logistical problems of the American army were, however, far from over. Indeed, by 1780, Trumbull and Connecticut were again called upon to rescue Washington's famished troops. While one often thinks of the winter at Valley Forge as the nadir of the morale of the American troops in the Revolutionary War, it is perhaps true that the winter of 1780 at Morristown, New Jersey, was an even more taxing period. Through the last half of 1779, the Commissary Department went through various alterations. Finally, the resignation of Jeremiah Wadsworth of Connecticut in December, 1779, removed from the Commissariat one of the few men with the ability and experience to keep the struggling department functioning. Soon afterwards, the provisioning of Washington's army came to an almost complete halt.

Washington had picked Morristown as the site of his winter encampment, as he had in the previous year, because of the accessibility of the location from both the South and New England. Washington expected substantial supplies from the South for the winter but sought to remain near the crucial Hudson Valley fortifications. Morristown selected, Washington's army began to move in for the winter in December, 1779.

From the beginning, the Morristown sojourn was a disaster. Little preparation had been made to shelter the troops before their arrival, and thus the poorly-provisioned men had to set to work to build log huts. The enterprise was made more complicated by the weather. The winter of 1778-1779 at Morristown had been a relatively mild one; that of 1779-1780 was extremely harsh. By the time the troops arrived in camp, two feet of snow already covered the ground. On January 3,

1780, by which time the huts were little more than half completed, the worst blizzard of the century hit the area.[72] With bitter cold winds lashing the camp, the drifts mounted to six feet. The scene was described by a military physician at the camp: ". . . the sufferings of the poor soldiers can scarcely be described; while on duty they are unavoidably exposed to all the inclemency of storms and severe ground; at night they have a bed of straw on the ground . . . . the soldiers are so enfeebled from hunger and cold, as to be almost unable to perform their military duty, or to labor constructing their huts."[73]

With the situation of his troops so desperate, Washington turned once again to Jonathan Trumbull of Connecticut. Washington wrote from Morristown on January 6, 1780:

> . . . The army has been near three months on a short allowance of bread; within a fortnight past almost perishing. They have been sometimes without bread, sometimes without meat; at no time with much of either, and often without both. They have borne their distress . . . with as much fortitude as human nature is capable of . . . [but] . . . the soldiery have in several instances plundered the neighboring inhabitants. . . . Without an immediate remedy this evil would soon become intolerable. . . . We are reduced to this alternative, either to let the army disband . . . or . . . to have recourse to a military impress. . . . Our situation is more than serious, it is alarming. I doubt not your excellency will view it in the same light and that the Legislature of the State of Connecticut will give fresh proof of their wisdom and zeal for the common cause, by their exertions upon the present occasion.[74]

Trumbull's response to Washington's emergency proved to be just as energetic as it had been during the Valley Forge crisis. The rider who brought the above letter to Trumbull arrived in Lebanon in the early afternoon.[75] The governor made provision for the man to rest for the evening. The next morning Trumbull gave the rider a message for Washington, detailing the exact quantity of provisions that would be forthcoming from Connecticut. Trumbull, in addition, noted the day and the hour that the foodstuffs would arrive in camp. Despite the difficulty of purchasing provisions from Connecticut farmers who were disgruntled with Continental paper[76] and in the face of frozen road and icy winds, the provisions, as Trumbull had promised, arrived on time to feed the starving troops.[77]

The provisions from Connecticut, along with the grain and cattle which Washington impressed from New Jersey farmers, terminated Washington's crisis at Morristown by the end of January, 1780.[78] Yet, in a sense it is true that Washington's logistical emergency did not really end until the summer of 1781. For, unlike the summer which followed Valley Forge, when the commissariat began to function well under Jeremiah Wadsworth, the American provisioning apparatus did not make a recovery in the spring and summer of 1780. The lack of credit of Congress and the various alterations which were instituted in the commissariat's purchasing procedures kept Washington in a precarious logistical situation until the spring and summer of 1781 when state requisitions and the management of provisioning by Robert Morris enabled Washington to begin the campaign which culminated in the great Yorktown victory.[79]

Thus, all through 1780 and the first half of 1781, the American troops were provisioned on an inconsistent and often unsatisfactory basis. Through this period, the disillusionment of the troops with insufficient food and worthless Continental paper brought mutiny in Continental regiments in May, 1780, and January, 1781.[80] Washington kept up a steady stream of provision's requests to Trumbull in Lebanon,[81] and the Connecticut governor maintained his reputation as a reliable source of logistical support by responding with much-needed supplies. In March, 1780, Trumbull supplied the Continental Army with 1,000 barrels of flour;[82] in September, 1780, with almost 600 head of cattle,[83] in November, 1780, with 1,500 barrels of beef, 25,000 hundredweight of beef, 25,000 gallons of rum, and 800 bushels of salt;[84] and, through 1781, when financial levies were required of the states to support the operations of the Continental Commissary, Trumbull succeeded in encouraging Connecticut to meet its fiscal responsibility to Congress.[85]

The contribution which Trumbull made to Continental provisioning in 1780 and 1781 was especially impressive in light of the growing distaste of the state's farmers to sell their grain and cattle for Continental currency. Continental paper money had, of course, been depreciating throughout the war, but by the late 1770s and early 1780s, its worthlessness had reached comic proportions. This was particularly true after Congress in March, 1780, devalued the currency to one-fortieth of face value. Naturally, little confidence thereafter remained in Continental paper. By 1781, President Stiles of Yale College noted that "At Philadelphia a Continental is 150 for 1. At New Haven 100 for 1. At Boston 130 for 1. All running into Confusion and Crisis as to money!"[86] While Connecticut's farmers were consequently unwilling to effect transactions for the dubious Continental paper,[87] they were displeased by the tardiness of Congress to appropriate funds to settle outstanding debts of the commissariat. There were scores of Connecticut farmers, for example, who had claims on the Commissary Department that went as far back as 1778-1779.[88] That it was the worthless Continental currency alone which made provisioning difficult was clearly demonstrated when Washington made his third special provisioning appeal to Trumbull and Connecticut.

Washington was notified in May, 1780, that a major French force under Rochambeau was to arrive in Newport, Rhode Island, in early summer.[89] Recognizing that the sputtering American commissariat was hardly in a position to undertake the supplying of the French, both Washington and Congress agreed that the provisioning would be left to the French commissary agents. Thus, the French Commissary, Louis Ethis de Corny, was given permission to secure provisions in whatever states he could and was assured that Congress would facilitate his task by furnishing letters of introduction to the state governors.[90] As it turned out, Congress need not have bothered with any other letter than that to Jonathan Trumbull of Connecticut.

In writing to Trumbull regarding the provisioning of the French at Newport, Washington assumed that the logistical task would be difficult and therefore made an urgent appeal to the Connecticut governor to take every possible measure to supply America's allies.[91] Similar letters were dispatched from Washington and Congress to William Greene, the governor of Rhode Island.[92] Trumbull, upon hearing that he was to be asked to provision a French force of 6,000 officers and men, wrote to Greene that the task would be an impossible one for his state to bear, but he nevertheless assured the Rhode Island governor that Connecticut would do her best.[93] Washington, Congress, Greene, and Trumbull were much too pessimistic about the task. In fact, the provisioning of Rochambeau's troops brought forth a monumental effort by Connecticut's farmers. Grain and cattle flowed from Connecticut to the French at Newport like water downhill. While Washington's troops were never sure from one day to the next that they would have sufficient food, Rochambeau's men and officers were enjoying hugh quantities of grain, cattle, and sheep.[94] It would be heartwarming to the memory of Lafayette to be able to explain the delightful French logistical situation as resulting from the deep sense of Franco-American unity that prevailed between Connecticut's Yankee farmers and the French army.

In truth, however, the outpouring of provisions from Connecticut to Newport was due to a more mundane factor—the French paid for their foodstuffs in gold. While the French commissaries had been instructed to utilize Continental paper in their transactions, they must have quickly realized that such a procedure, while comforting to Congress, would not be effective in feeding their troops. From the outset of their dealings with New England farmers, consequently, the French offered specie. Once the Connecticut sons learned that they would not have to part with grain and livestock for Continental paper or certificates, they literally glutted the French storehouses with provisions. Indeed, the joys of dealing with the French were reputed to be so profitable that men who were laboring in the state and national commissariats fled from their posts to become agents for Rochambeau. All in all, then, Connecticut responded with energy and dispatch to Washington's appeal to provision the force of Rochambeau at Newport.

While it is true that the motivation of Connecticut's farmers in this circumstance was more covetous than patriotic, the fact remains that once again Connecticut, under the direction of Governor Trumbull, had succeeded in making a major contribution to the American military effort.

Indeed, although the efforts of Trumbull and Connecticut in the Valley Forge, Morristown, and Newport episodes were particularly important for the maintenance of both American and French forces, it must be noted that these were but three occasions when Connecticut was called upon to make an extraordinary contribution to America's military structure. Throughout the years of the Revolutionary War, Trumbull was responsible for overseeing the provisioning of all the state troops both in militia and Continental regiments. Utilizing the agricultural resources of Connecticut and supervising the generally efficient state commissariat, Trumbull, working with his Council of Safety, was able to conduct a logistical operation that was perhaps the most productive of any American state during the war.[95] Further, Trumbull was, in addition, the director of another phase of Connecticut's wartime activities that proved to be especially crucial in determining Washington's ultimate victory—the production of weapons and gunpowder.

America entered the Revolutionary War with few facilities for the manufacture of gunpowder. In fact, it has been estimated that some 90 per cent of the powder used by American troops in the first two and a half years of the war came from Europe.[96] While imported powder continued to exercise a crucial role throughout the war, some states, such as Connecticut, made an effort to produce the commodity. Under the direction of Trumbull and the Council of Safety,[97] Connecticut offered a bounty for the production of powder in the first year of the war.[98] Soon mills were operating in East Hartford, Windham, New Haven, Stratford, Glastonbury, and Salisbury.[99] The state appointed inspectors to oversee the quality of the production of the mills[100] and required that mill operators post a bond of £2,000 as security against misuse of the powder produced.[101] Nevertheless, Connecticut's production of gunpowder was limited throughout the Revolutionary War by insufficient supplies of saltpeter and sulphur. Generally, the state itself secured these commodities through its commissariat and then transferred them to the various mill operators.[102] Occasionally, however, a mill owner was given permission to secure his needed saltpeter directly from Boston or Providence.[103] Despite the difficulty involved in the accumulation of saltpeter and sulphur, Connecticut was able during the war to provide gunpowder to the American forces at Ticonderoga (1775),[104] Cambridge (1775),[105] Fish Kill (1781),[106] and Horseneck (1781).[107] The bulk of the state-produced gunpowder, however, was dispatched to those Connecticut towns, i.e., Stratford, New

50

Haven, Groton, Norwich, and New London, which were apprehensive of British attacks from either New York or the sea.[108]

Connecticut made a more important contribution under Governor Trumbull to the Continental Army with its guns than it did with its powder. Connecticut was fortunate in 1775 in having a number of skilled craftsmen who had already distinguished themselves in the field of gunmaking. These men were induced to increase their production by a bounty of five shillings per gun.[109] These craftsmen, especially in Mansfield, Windham, and Goshen, were able to produce sufficient guns so that the Connecticut men sent to the Continental Army generally were armed. Overshadowing the efforts of Connecticut's gunsmiths, however, was the crucial production of cannon at the Salisbury foundry.

The operation was taken over by the Connecticut General Assembly at the beginning of the war when the owner, a suspected Tory, fled to Great Britain. The actual overseeing of the foundry's operation was handled by Governor Trumbull and the Council of Safety.[110] Since the American forces were so short of heavy weapons during the early years of the war, Trumbull, working with his council, devoted considerable attention to the management of the Salisbury operation.[111] With the production of the foundry increasing, and its direction therefore becoming a more complicated task, the General Assembly in 1776 and 1777 provided for a committee of four to handle its operation. Nevertheless, Trumbull and the council throughout the war still were responsible for a multitude of tasks that were crucial for the functioning of the Salisbury enterprise. Much of the provisioning of the foundry was effected by special orders to the Connecticut commissariat which originated in Lebanon.[112] The governor and the council granted the Salisbury managers permission to impress such needed materials as wood,[113] and they did everything possible to provide the foundry with brimstone and salt when the foundry committee was unable to secure them.[114] The General Assembly cooperated actively in maintaining the foundry by providing military exemptions for its workers[115] and by appropriating funds regularly for the expenses of the operation.[116] In the last years of the war, the Salisbury foundry was leased by the state to mangers who paid a modest rent to the state treasury. The effort which was made regarding Salisbury proved to be most significant for the American cause. Salisbury cannon went to General Schuyler in the Northern Department in the spring of 1777.[117] More generally, however, cannon, grape shot, and round shot from Salisbury were sent to arm such Connecticut towns as Norwalk, New Haven, Greenwich, Stamford, Guilford, Newfield, New London, Norwich, and Wallingford.[118] If these towns had not been so fortunate as to be protected by the products from Salisbury, it is likely that Connecticut would have felt more keenly than she did the lash of the British sword, a circumstance which inevitably would have made the state considerably less capable of making its logistical contributions to the Continental Army.[119]

While Trumbull, with the council and the General Assembly, was laboring to provide the American forces with provisions, powder, and weapons, he, as was true of all the state governors, was constantly being inundated by appeals from the military and Congress for troops. As he had regarding all Continental requests made of him, Trumbull labored energetically to raise troops for the American cause. While proclamations were sufficient in the opening years of the war to bring forth Connecticut sons for state and Continental service, by 1777, Trumbull and the General Assembly had to resort to bounties to insure that the state would have sufficient manpower for militia and national service.[120] On the whole, Connecticut's manpower contribution was impressive. With a total population of 200,000, the state had almost 40,000 of her sons see military service of some sort.[121] Connecticut troops were at most of the significant engagements, especially those in the north, of the Revolutionary War—the northern campaign (1775-1776), Boston (1775-1776), Long Island (1776), White Plains (1776), Trenton (1776), Saratoga (1777), Germantown (1777), Stony Point (1779), and Yorktown (1781).[122]

Yet, although the activity of Connecticut's troops was certainly substantial, it must be said that, like most American troops during the Revolutionary War, they demonstrated relatively little staying power. Desertion and absenteeism proved to be the bane of Washington throughout the war, and the sons of Connecticut were no better than most in their haste to return to home and fireside. Philip Schuyler reported to Trumbull in October, 1775, that the Connecticut troops at Ticonderoga had "melted away."[123] Although Trumbull at first disputed Schuyler's charge, he soon realized its validity and wrote a mild letter to Congress explaining that the men departed believing that their obligation terminated with the expiration of their enlistment period.[124] That the Ticonderoga affair was not an isolated happening was demonstrated after the American loss at the Battle of Long Island in 1776. Connecticut troops fled in droves, with an estimated 6,000 of the 8,000 Connecticut militiamen deserting. An observer wrote that ". . . the officers and Men belonging to the Militia behaved extremely ill; and Officers of all Ranks and Privates kept deserting and running off in a most Shameful Scandalous Manner; and some were taken sick and a great Many more pretended to be so."[125]

Probably recognizing that punishment to deserters would only hinder the state in its task of filling its quotas of troops, Connecticut took no punitive action against them. The only measures enacted by the General Assembly regarding the subject were acts in 1776 and 1777 providing for pardons for those who were willing to reassume their military obligations.[126] Such a permissive policy was undoubtedly an indication of the increasing difficulty as the war continued in maintaining the militia and Continental regiments for which Connecticut was responsible. Trumbull wrote to Washington often on the problems involved in raising troops,[127] but he discussed the subject at some length in February, 1777. Trumbull wrote that the men of Connecticut were developing a "distrust for the service" resulting from the lack of food, clothing, shelter, and pay which they experienced in the Continental service. He mused that while bounties either of money or land might induce men to enlist for the three-year period Washington wanted, the task of recruitment in Connecticut would be difficult.[128] Shortly afterwards, the state passed its first bounty legislation, but for the remainder of the war Connecticut had a most trying time in keeping its Continental strength at ten infantry regiments, one cavalry regiment, and five artillery companies.[129] The combination of infrequent pay and the widespread resentment that existed in Revolutionary America against military discipline made the task of maintaining an adequate military force perhaps the most perplexing one which Trumbull, as well as every other major political and military leader, confronted during the Revolutionary War.

Yet, an examination of the contributions which Jonathan Trumbull made to American military success must not be such as to ignore the Connecticut governor's activities regarding the establishment of a functioning government, without which the men of Washington would have been more undernourished and poorly-equipped than they were. The creation of government, even under tranquil and calm circumstances, has always been one of man's most taxing functions. To attempt to establish government among thirteen separate and often conflicting units while the society was confronted with an armed threat to its very existence raised conflicts that would have made the residents of Olympus shudder. That, of course, was exactly what the youthful American state had to do following the Declaration of Independence. Despite differences in social organization, economic patterns, ethnic and racial population compositions, and philosophical and theological inclinations, the struggling Americans were successful in bringing forth a framework of government in the Articles of Confederation, which, although not without blemishes, laid the groundwork for the development of an enduring republic. No American in the Revolutionary era was a more ardent supporter of national political organization than was Jonathan Trumbull of Connecticut.

Although Connecticut had demonstrated a rigid respect for its tradition of political autonomy during the evolving Anglo-American controversy of the 1760s and 1770s, the state followed an essentially nationalistic course during the period of the evolution of the Articles of Confederation.[130] Connecticut did not, of course, ignore her own interests, but she did, in moments of decision, regard matters of national organization and security as more crucial than those of state or sectional concern. Even before independence, opinion in the state inclined toward a movement for the creation of a national system of government. In April, 1776, the *Connecticut Courant* declared that

> An American state or empire is much talked of; the materials of which it is to be formed are a number of flourishing colonies and possessions, heretofore independent of each other; the materials are noble and the building vast. The master builders ought to look to the foundation, that is to support and hold together this mighty fabric, that it be surely laid and . . . cemented . . . the universal voice is therefore, that there must be as the foundation corner of the American independency, an explicit league and covenant . . . containing articles of confederation, formed and solemnly confirmed by all the colonies, as the bond of this union and basis of their government.[131]

That the *Courant* statement was representative of considerably more than the editor's viewpoint was demonstrated some two months later when the Connecticut General Assembly resolved that the state's delegation to Congress should not only support American independence but should as well "move and promote, as fast as may be convenient, a regular and permanent Plan of Union and Confederation for the Colonies, for the security and preservation of their just rights and liberties, and for mutual defence and security."[132]

At Philadelphia, the debate on the proposal for confederation which was prepared by a committee headed by John Dickinson in June, 1776, waxed until November, 1777.[133] The Connecticut delegates found themselves immersed in two controversies that endangered continental union. First, the larger states, *e. g*, Virginia, pushed for representation based on population. Connecticut, joining with the smaller states, demanded that there be an equal voice for all states in the proposed national framework. Roger Sherman held that delegates represented states, not individuals, and he warned that if proportional representation were adopted, the three largest states of Virginia, New York, and Pennsylvania would have enough votes to control the Congress but would, nevertheless, have insufficient strength "to carry these votes into execution."[134] Finally, the Connecticut view held as the issue was resolved on the side of equal voting strength in Congress for all states.[135] The conclave, however, was still bitterly divided on the basis on which war costs were to be apportioned. The New England delegates generally sought population as the principal basis; the Connecticut delegates took this position, reflecting the views of Trumbull and the General Assembly.[136] Delegates from the southern and middle states, however, put forward the proposition that the value of land and improvements thereon be used rather than population.[137]

While northern delegates objected to the proposal, since lands in their states had higher values than those to the south, and because it eliminated from consideration the Negro slaves which were the most valuable property in the southern states, they finally agreed to the proposal when it was clear that without it there would be no confederation. Finally, on November 15, 1777, the Congress agreed on the constructed Articles of Confederation and ordered 300 copies distributed to the state delegations.[138] Now, the issues rested with the states, all of which had to ratify if the Articles were to be adopted.

Once the copies of the Articles were dispatched to Connecticut, the hand of Trumbull appeared as the guiding force in the action of the state. While Jonathan Trumbull was outdistanced by no man in his desire to see the American nation politically unified in order to shoulder its divine mission,[139] his approach to Connecticut's examination of the Articles manifested a sure perception of the state's political traditions. Himself immersed in the historic, Connecticut, town-meeting atmosphere, Trumbull appeared to recognize that the more searching the public debate on the Articles, the more likely there would be popular commitment to the Confederation.[140] He therefore decided to distribute the proposal directly to the state's freemen *via* the town selectmen rather than to delay public discussion until the Articles were presented to the next session of the General Assembly. Thus, on December 15, 1777, Trumbull drafted a circular letter to Connecticut's selectmen, requesting that they communicate the Articles of Confederation "to the inhabitants in Town Meeting . . . so that their sense thereon may be known."[141] His Council of Safety sitting in Lebanon having approved of Trumbull's inclination,[142] copies of the Articles were printed and distributed throughout the state by the end of the month.[143]

Generally, the reaction of the towns which was communicated to the General Assembly was positive.[144] The most unpopular feature of the document was the provision, opposed by New England at Philadelphia, for the apportionment of the war costs on the basis of land and buildings thereon.[145] A number of towns offered alternatives such as apportioning taxes on the basis of all property or according to population.[146] Another alteration suggested was that the freemen of the state, rather than the General Assembly, be responsible for the designation of Connecticut's representatives to Congress.[147] Finally, two towns had their own particular objections to the Articles of Confederation. Norwalk held that the system for determining the state quota of Continental troops on the basis of white population was "not so just and Equitable as may be devised," and Farmington asserted that the requirement of a nine-state majority on certain questions in congressional voting was not adequate protection for Connecticut and New England against a combination of "western" and southern states.[148]

Still in all, when the General Assembly met in January, 1778, the legislators found that most of the state's freemen favored ratification of the Articles.

The reaction of the towns being essentially positive, the numbers of the General Assembly were toward immediate ratification. Trumbull, however, enjoined measured action, noting that "A Matter of this Importance seldom presents itself—and should never be determined but with the utmost Caution and Candor."[149] The Assembly, reflecting the nationalistic drive which dominated Connecticut public opinion,[150] ignored the governor and discussed and approved without qualification the proposal from Philadelphia.[151] The assistants of the upper house, on the other hand, more under the governor's influence, encouraged more thoughtful examination of the Articles by rejecting this ratification of the deputies and deferring consideration of the Articles until the next month's Assembly session.[152]

The measured approach of Trumbull and the assistants brought dividends during the February, 1778, session of the General Assembly, for the members of the House of Representatives effected a searching examination of the Articles of Confederation. While the deputies held that the framework of government proposed was "in general well adapted to cement and preserve the union of States [and] to secure their freedom and independence and promote their general welfare," two amendments were approved. First, that population, favored by Connecticut's towns and its delegates to Congress, be used rather than land values as a basis for taxation. Too, the House of Representatives were troubled by a provision in the Articles which gave Congress the power to appoint officers in the army and navy of the United States, make regulations for the operation of the military, and direct all military activities. Reflecting that Anglo-Saxon fear of a standing military establishment, the deputies approved an amendment "that no standing army shall be kept by the United States in time of peace, nor any officers or pensioners kept in pay unless they were in actual service . . . or disabled veterans."[153] While the two amendments were to be conditions of Connecticut's ratification, the Assembly's basic support of prompt adoption was reflected in its direction that Congress be allowed to establish the specifics of the alterations proposed, and that the state congressional delegates be instructed "to agree to and ratify . . . the Articles of Confederation with such amendments, if any be, as by them in conjunction with the Delegates of the other States in Congress shall be thought proper."[154]

Taking their cue from the Assembly's resolution, the Connecticut delegates in Congress were supportive of the prompt adoption of the Articles of Confederation. Although Congress rejected all proposed amendments to the documents, the Connecticut delegates in July, 1778, voted to approve the Articles of Confederation.[155] By January,

1779, twelve states had signed the Articles, with but Maryland remaining out of the fold. Maryland's recalcitrance was based upon its unwillingness to approve the Articles until all the states, especially Virginia, had ceded to the United States their claims to the territory between the Alleghenies and the Mississippi.[156] Trumbull was in no mood to see the proposed instrument of American union fail of ratification because of one state. He wrote to the Connecticut delegates in Congress in February, 1779, that the path to follow was to establish the Confederation and let Maryland sulk if she wished.[157] Trumbull's nationalistic impatience was shared by the General Assembly. In April, 1779, the Connecticut Assembly resolved to instruct the state's congressional delegation to propose the establishment of the Confederation at once, with Maryland given the option of joining later.[158]

Since the Connecticut proposal to establish the Confederation without Maryland was not carried in Congress,[159] the state tried another approach to hastening adoption. Impressed with Maryland's insistence upon all states ceding to Congress their western land claims, the Connecticut General Assembly in October, 1780, supported a congressional move toward cession of land claims by granting to the states which would confederate "joint right of soil to the vacant lands within her charter claim westward of the Susquehannah Purchase, and eastward of the Mississippi."[160] Congress subsequently forced the state to make its cession without qualification regarding the claim in the Wyoming Valley.[161] Finally, by 1781, when New York and Virginia had given up their western claims and Maryland was growing apprehensive regarding British arms in the southern states, Maryland at last effected the establishment of the Confederation by its ratification of the Articles. With Trumbull and Connecticut serving as an encouraging force, the Gordian knot had been untied and an American union established. Unfortunately, the evolution of the Confederation was not a remedy for the nation's political ills.

Indeed, the years from 1777, when the American states began their move toward adoption of the Articles of Confederation, were ones in which national political cohesiveness appeared to be less and less possible in the United States. Congress limped along during the war, weakened by intrigue, factionalism, profiteering in procuring army supplies, speculation on the basis of secret information, and ever-present instances of geographical and philosophical division. Having no power, and often no inclination, to demand regular financial and logistical support from the states, Congress frequently resembled an important debating society in which even the members were bored with the proceedings. Connecticut's delegates in Congress wrote to Trumbull of the depressing inactivity. Titus Hosmer, in August, 1778, noted that Congress seemed paralyzed by the sectional hostility beween the northern and southern states. The result of the impasse was that members regarded attendance at meetings as insignificant. Only trivia, according to Hosmer, was given attention by the august body.[162] As such reports continued to come to Lebanon,[163] Trumbull became increasingly impatient. The governor wrote the state delegation in October, 1778, that he was disturbed at the accounts he had received. He urged Connecticut's representatives to encourage Congress to meet its responsibilities by confronting the crucial questions which plagued the nation.[164] Of the questions which Trumbull had in mind, none was more significant than that of national finances.

Caught between a shortage of specie in Revolutionary America and its own lack of power to lay taxes upon the states, Congress, in 1775, resorted to an emission of £3,000,000 in paper money to finance the war. While there was experimentation in Philadelphia regarding the utilization of popular loans and lotteries, Congress stuck essentially to the paper money expediency. By 1780, after 37 emissions, the total amount of paper money circulation was over $240,000,000. The latter figure, however, represented only the face value of the currency; as a result of the constant depreciation which accompanied the emissions, the Continental paper in specie was estimated to be worth no more than $5,000,000.[165]

Many Americans, including Jonathan Trumbull, watched hopelessly between 1775 and 1780 as the Continental notes depreciated, making it a completely fruitless medium for the purchase of military supplies and provisions. Trumbull had seen the impossibility of the currency situation as Connecticut farmers hoarded their produce when visited by state and national commissary agents who sought to exchange the worthless paper for grain and cattle. Too, Trumbull's letters from the Connecticut delegation in Congress indicated that the depreciation of Continental paper was a national rather than just a state problem. Roger Sherman, for example, wrote in 1778 that the declining purchasing power of the paper money had effected uncontrollable inflation in Philadelphia, with prices four to six times what they had been at the time of the Coercive Acts.[166] Trumbull's hard money position became even more resolute as he received such information. He wrote time after time to Congress, urging that it secure its paper money by taxation and foreign loans, for the continuation of emissions of rapidly-depreciating Continental paper could only lead to a worsening of the American fiscal morass.[167]

Trumbull's letters had little impact upon affairs at Philadelphia, where, between 1779 and 1781, Congress was involved in a "nightmare of frenzied finance."[168] Bills of exchange were issued on foreign ministers in the expectation that by the time the bills were presented, the diplomats could have borrowed funds to pay for them.[169] The paper money problem continued with another $125,000,000 being issued; the situation had become so desperate, however, that the purchasing power of the new emission was less than $6,000,000.[170] Finally, in one last gamble to halt the depreciation, Congress, in 1780, devalued all the outstanding paper at 40 to 1, thereby reducing $200,000,000 to $5,000,000.[171] The gamble failed. Soon the $5,000,000 depreciated out of circulation, and Congress had to virtually admit its impotence by allowing the Quartermaster and Commissary Departments to take whatever it needed from the populace in exchange for notes promising eventual payment from "the United States in Congress."[172] The citizenry embittered by impressment, Congress, in 1780 and early 1781, in effect abandoned its financial responsibilities and pleaded with the states to assume the financial burden of current pay, arrears, and compensation for currency depreciation.[173] The states, including Connecticut under Trumbull, were the only barrier left throughout 1780 to stem the tide of American financial collapse. Their efforts, based on increased taxation, were successful in keeping the American forces in the field, but the cost was high—by the end of 1780, most of them joined Congress in a state of finanical exhaustion.[174]

And yet, the bitter situation was not without positive results. By early 1781 the extent and seriousness of the financial collapse of both Congress and the states led to the emergence of a nationalist-oriented group of businessmen and statesmen. Determined that the emerging nation was not to be engulfed by a tidal wave of fiscal chaos, men such as Robert Livingston, James Duane, James Wilson, and John Sullivan collaborated to hammer out a program that would provide the nation with a substantial fiscal base. In February, 1781, Congress thus moved toward the establishment of a permanent source of income for itself by asking the states for the power to levy an impost of five per cent on goods imported into the United States.[175] The same nationalistic impulse was responsible some two weeks later for congressional reorganization of its administrative departments, with the crucial position of superintendent of financing going to the fiscally-sound, Philadelphia merchant, Robert Morris.[176]

While the Connecticut delegation to Congress, as well as the governor in Lebanon, proved to be more than willing to witness the reinforcement of national political strength which the passage of the impost by the states would effect, the impost question raised a churning political debate in Connecticut. The essentially nationalistic political consensus which had existed in Connecticut through most of the war began to crack in the debate over the impost. Elements in and out of the General Assembly used the impost proposal to question the trend toward increased power and financial independence by the Congress. The state's aging governor, growing tired and burdened by his labors in the cause of American nationhood, would enjoy perhaps his most respected hour as he responded to this manifestation of political provincialism. Both the provincialism and Trumbull's reaction to it, however, can only be understood within the context of an examination of Jonathan Trumbull's administration of Connecticut during the Revolutionary War.

War Governor: State Affairs

W HILE Jonathan Trumbull is perhaps best remembered for his efforts on behalf of the military and political success of the emerging American nation during the Revolutionary War, his contributions to the United States were possible only insofar as he was able to govern the state of Connecticut effectively during the turbulent war years. Challenged by the governmental alteration which was necessitated by the demands of the war, threatened by British troops in New York, forced to establish unprecedented economic controls in order to mobilize the state's military and logistical resources, and faced with increasing popular resistance to the centralization of both state and national power which the war demanded, Trumbull from 1775 to 1783 managed to administer the affairs of Connecticut with minimum internal dislocation and within maximum realization of the state's potential contribution to the establishment of American independence.[1]

Certainly a factor which contributed to Trumbull's effectiveness was the essential continuity which characterized Connecticut government during the transition from colony to state. As the only governor serving in 1775 who continued in office after independence, Trumbull did not face the crushing task of acquainting himself with his office while mobilizing for war.[2] As important, Trumbull was fortunate during the early years of the war in not having to preside over a basic reconstruction of Connecticut's government. Those who assumed the governorships of states of former royal or proprietary colonies had, in effect, to fight the war while they were immersed in the complex task of constitution-making.[3] Connecticut, as did her sister corporate colony, Rhode Island,[4] became an independent American state with a minimum of constitutional alteration.

Although Trumbull and Connecticut escaped the necessity of constitutional transformation, neither was able to function during the Revolutionary War without political adjustments. The principal political alteration which Connecticut experienced in the war years involved a dimunition of the power of the General Assembly.[5] Throughout Connecticut's history, the most potent organ of government had been the legislative branch. The Chamber of Deputies and the Council of Assistants controlled all aspects of church-state relations, ruled over qualifications and procedures for elections, regulated the militia, determined county boundaries, and supervised the political and economic affairs of the colony's towns.

The governor was, by comparison, a minor element in the government of Connecticut. The office did, it is true, carry with it tremendous prestige. It was generally regarded as the political prize which came to a man after literally a lifetime of sustained public service. Becoming governor, a Connecticut son could count upon holding the office until he was removed by incapacity or death.[6] In fact, however, the governor of colonial Connecticut did not exercise much influence in government. He issued proclamations for fast days and thanksgiving occasions, signed appointments for judicial and militia posts, and named rather insignificant officeholders such as county sheriffs. The most demanding and honorific positions in the civil and military lists were filled by appointees of the Chamber of Deputies and the council. Furthermore, the governor had little involvement in the legislative process. The Revolutionary War, and the political acumen of Jonathan Trumbull, effected a significant transformation of the relative importance of the governor and the Assembly.

The principal factor in the shift in power from the Assembly to the governor was the military demands of the Revolutionary War. While Governor Trumbull was constitutionally designated as commander of the state's militia, the General Assembly was traditionally empowered to regulate the actual operation of Connecticut's military forces. By the second month of the Revolutionary War, however, it was apparent to the Connecticut lawmakers that the General Assembly, meeting twice a year for brief one-month sessions, was hardly capable of overseeing the raising, officering, provisioning, and directing of the state's troops for militia and Continental duty. Jealous, nevertheless, of its constitutional prerogatives, the members of the Assembly were unwilling to solve the dilemma by empowering the governor to conduct military affairs while the legislature was not in session.[7] The solution decided upon was the establishment of a "Committee of Safety" composed of Assembly members which would *aid* the governor. Thus, in May, 1775, the General Assembly established a committee "to assist the Governor when the Assembly was not in session, to direct the marches and stations of the soldiers enlisted for the defense of the colony, or any part of them as they should judge proper, and supply with every matter and thing that should be needful for the defense of the colony."[8] By this step, the General Assembly hoped to maintain its authority and at the same time meet its military responsibilities.

If events in Connecticut had followed the pattern of those in most other states, the Committee of Safety would indeed have served as a check upon the military activities of the governor. In state after state, such committees were established to oversee military affairs while the legislature was not in session.[9] Although the committees were usually given extensive authority to care for the "safety of the public," their effectiveness was often limited by the overbearing control of the legislatures. Members of the committees were kept on a short rein by the tactic of limited tenure established by the assemblies. Too, the committees themselves could be restructured or even abolished by the will of the legislature. Finally, the committees were hampered in carrying out their military responsibilities by constant meddling on the part of the assemblies. The result, of course, was that the military efforts of a number of states were confused and inept.[10] In Connecticut, however, the Committee of Safety proved to be a most effective instrument throughout the Revolutionary War.[11]

The committee, which was in existence from May, 1775, until October, 1783, was primarily charged with the supervision of the state's military and naval forces.[12] The most difficult task of Trumbull and the Committee of Safety in this context was the appointment of the Connecticut troops in the face of varied calls. Rarely throughout the war was the committee not faced with endless troops requisitions for the Continental service. At the same time, the western and coastal towns of Connecticut, fearful of British thrusts from New York or the sea, were usually clamoring for additional militia. The calls of the latter were particularly urgent after the British attack on Danbury in April, 1777.

While Trumbull and the committee had received calls for troops from the western and coastal towns before 1777, the attack on Danbury increased the apprehension among town selectmen and militia officers. In the months after Danbury, Trumbull was repeatedly told that the militia in western Connecticut would be completely unable to ward off any significant British assault.[13]

Having received the news of the Danbury attack, Trumbull dispatched to Washington a detailed account of the disaster. Noting that the raid had cost the Americans heavily in provisions—1,700 barrels of pork, 50 barrels of beef, 700 bushels of wheat, 1,700 bushels of corn, as well as 1,600 tents—Trumbull throughout May, 1777, pleaded with the general for Continental support for Connecticut.[14] Washington, recognizing the pressure that Trumbull was under from the towns, wrote frankly that he would certainly come to the aid of Connecticut more promptly than he would for other areas, but that the scattering of the Continental force was the very result that the British sought by such attacks as that on Danbury. Therefore, Washington would have to refuse the request and hope that Trumbull and Connecticut would be able to provide for the protection of the state.[15]

Trumbull, who as much as any governor recognized that the Continental consideration had to take precedence over a single state's security,[16] wrote to Washington that he understood the reason for the general's refusal and would endeavor to meet Connecticut's troop needs by utilization of the militia.[17] That, of course, was more easily said than done, for the remaining years of the war brought repeated requests from western and coastal towns for troops and arms.[18] Trumbull subsequently sought support from the Continental forces,[19] but for the most part he utilized the physical and logistical resources of Connecticut for the state's defense. Trumbull and the Committee of Safety frequently shuffled troops from one location to another to anticipate possible enemy thrusts.[20]

While the British were able to mount raids into Connecticut in 1779 and 1781, the strategic importance of these thrusts was essentially limited. Despite the assaults, Connecticut was able to continue to serve throughout the Revolutionary War as a principal source of provisions for Washington's troops. That the state was able to escape so relatively lightly the British sword and torch must be regarded, at least in part, as an indication of Connecticut's general military readiness under the direction of Governor Trumbull and the Committee of Safety. It is true that the Connecticut forces were not able to block the British in New York from intrusions in the state, but, more significantly, the Connecticut Militia was sufficiently effective to prevent any *major* British invasion.

The military charge of Governor Trumbull and the Committee of Safety also included supervision of the state's small but potent fleet.[21] During the Revolutionary War, Connecticut floated a total of thirteen vessels, including brigantines, ships, sloops, schooners, and row galleys.[22] Trumbull and the Committee of Safety had direct control of the vessels and orders were issued from Lebanon to raise crews, assign officers, and arm and provision.[23] Many of the details, especially regarding the provisioning of the vessels, were delegated to the state's naval agents, Nathaniel Shaw of New London and Samuel Eliot, Jr., of Boston.

While Nathaniel Shaw conducted well the provisioning and repairing of Connecticut vessels at New London,[24] the later years of the war made that port less useful, as the British in New York were able to keep a frequent watch. Therefore, more and more of the state's ships came to use Boston for provisioning and refitting. There, Samuel Eliot, Jr., did a thorough job not only in providing ample stores and arranging for repairs,[25] but also in serving as liaison between Governor Trumbull and the Committee of Safety and the Continental Navy Board. The correspondence indicates, as one might expect, that Trumbull cooperated fully with the board, revising his orders in light of the board's suggested sailing plans.[26] Eliot was also delegated by the authorities in Lebanon to handle the auction of captured vessels. Eliot generally sent along to Trumbull and the Committee of Safety the proceeds of the auctions,[27] but occasionally, on order from Lebanon, he purchased items, such as lead and salt, which were scarce in Connecticut.[28]

Although the Connecticut naval operation was perhaps not the most polished and sophisticated, the state's fleet was not without honors during the Revolutionary War. The *Oliver Cromwell*, the largest of the state's vessels, was a full-rigged ship which took nine enemy prizes between 1777 and 1779, the most valuable of which was the brig *Honour* which carried a cargo worth £10,000.[29] The *Defence*, another full-rigged Connecticut ship, was even more successful. She took thirteen British ships, including three troop transports, before she was broken on a reef trying to limp back to New London in 1779.[30] Nor did the Connecticut vessels confine their attacks to merchantmen and transports. The *Trumbull*, a 36-gun frigate of 700 tons, built in Connecticut and later sailed for the Continental Navy, fought an unflinching three-hour battle with the British man-of-war *Watt* and more than held her own.[31] All in all, the Connecticut fleet was responsible for capturing over 40 enemy vessels[32] and thus rendered significant service to the Continental cause.[33]

Perhaps an even more formidable naval weapon of Governor Trumbull and the Committee of Safety was the privateering activity of state vessels. Connecticut merchant-shipowners, finding their ships and crews idled by the disruption of normal trading patterns and by the increasingly-stringent British blockade, were not unhappy to see the passage of continental and state legislation to legalize privateering. In the fall of 1775 and the spring of 1776, Congress established provisions for both itself and the states to commission privateers.[34] The Connecticut General Assembly took the cue from Congress, and in May, 1776, authorized Governor Trumbull to issue commissions "for Private Ships of War."[35] The sons of Connecticut were eager to combine their patriotic and acquisitive[36] impulses, and the result was that between 200 and 300 state privateers sailed during the Revolutionary War from ports such as New London, New Haven, Wethersfield, Hartford, Saybrook, and East Haddam.[37] While the especially tight British blockade of New England kept Connecticut privateering at a minimum during 1776 and 1777,[38] the shift of British military interest southward in 1778 signaled the flowering of state privateering activity. The high tide came in the period 1779-1780, with New London serving as the state's favorite privateering port. Although the signing of commissions for privateers was still another of the endless tasks for which Trumbull of Lebanon was responsible during the Revolutionary War,[39] at least the governor and his Committee of Safety could take pleasure in the record of Connecticut's privateers. They were able to take as prizes over 500 British merchantmen,[40] a blow, along with the British prizes taken by privateers commissioned by Congress and other states,[41] which inclined British merchants to regard George III's continued prosecution of the Revolutionary War with less than elation.

It would appear, then, that Trumbull and the Committee of Safety were generally able to dicharge their military responsibilities during the Revolutionary War with uncommon dispatch and success. That the governor and the Committee of Safety were able to work effectively in Connecticut, as they were often unable to do in a number of states, must be related to the public trust in which Jonathan Trumbull was held. While in some states the Committee of Safety acted as a watchdog on the governor and in the process significantly impeded the war effort, in Connecticut there was complete harmony between Governor Trumbull and the members of the Committee of Safety. Not once in the entire course of the war were the decisions made at Lebanon the cause for opposition among the members of the committee or the members of the General Assembly, the body to which the Committee of Safety was constitutionally responsible. In fact, the evidence indicates that the Committee of Safety was altogether too willing to let Governor Trumbull carry the administrative burden alone. Trumbull's correspondence with the committee members often contained pleas that they attend the Lebanon meetings.[42] Although the members usually did respond by attending, the wartime correspondence of Jonathan Trumbull reveals that *he*, in effect, carried on the Connecticut war effort. Day after day, through personal tragedy, and through news of military defeat, financial chaos, and political confusion at Philadelphia, Jonathan Trumbull sat at his desk in the "War Office" and turned out the directives, and occasionally pleas, that kept the Connecticut war effort functioning until ultimate victory was achieved. The old man came to be something of a comic figure to the sophisticated visitors, especially the French, who passed through Lebanon during the war. Remarks were made about the short, unimposing governor whose conversation was saturated with biblical exhortations. Yet, the smiles never lingered very long, for this Old Testament patriarch never appeared anachronistic when the time came for performance. His quotas were always filled on time. He was the man to whom Washington turned when the shaky Continental Army was on the point of dissolution. In time, as the French came to appreciate the man's total commitment to victory, it was said that "when Louis XV asked Vergennes at Constantinople to send the Sultan's head, Vergennes replied that it would be a very delicate and difficult matter but would nevertheless send the head; Trumbull would not have even discussed the difficulty involved, he would have just sent the head."[43]

And yet, Jonathan Trumbull's secure tenure as war governor was based on more than just his efficient direction of the state's war effort and his association with the Connecticut establishment. Indeed, perhaps the most commendable, and generally recognized,[44] feature of his wartime administration was his wise and compassionate management of a number of vexing matters. The governor's handling of Connecticut's Tories, British prisoners of war, and the state's trade embargo reveals the understanding and sophistication which Jonathan Trumbull applied to his decisions.

Connecticut's Tories had little influence in the Revolutionary era. By the winter of 1774-1775, Connecticut's Whigs had begun a series of assaults on those lukewarm or actually hostile to the Patriot cause. With the news of Lexington and Concord, the Whigs became even more energetic in quieting and punishing Tories. Those who drank tea, failed to participate in days of patriotic fasting and thanksgiving, or actually spoke out against the political direction of the colony were subjected at worst to brutal physical assaults which often included tar and feathers and at the least to social isolation.[45] Not content with anti-Tory activity on the local level, Whigs in towns throughout Connecticut appealed to the General Assembly to enact a comprehensive measure to contain the colony's Tories.[46]

Despite the rising anti-Tory tide, Governor Trumbull approached the matter of legislation with caution. Perhaps unwilling to suggest definitive action until he was certain that the Whig cause would have the support of the rest of the American colonies, Trumbull spoke to the October, 1775, session of the General Assembly of "The Sword of Civil War" hanging over America, but he did not, at that time, call for legislation regarding Connecticut's Tories.[47] Other Connecticut Whigs were less inclined toward moderation. Extra-legal Patriot groups set about disarming those with known Loyalist views in western Connecticut. Tories in Newtown, Redding, Danbury, Ridgefield, Woodbury, and Derby were disarmed in what a Whig called "a quiet Manner with many Gentlemen of the first Character in the Country."[48] The movement toward anti-Tory legislation in Connecticut was reinforced in November, 1775, when Washington wrote to Trumbull urging that those who "will be active against us" be seized.[49] Finally, Connecticut's Tories helped those Whigs who were calling for legislation by maintaining throughout the fall of 1775 an outspoken loyalty to king and empire.[50]

With mounting public support, Washington's encouragement, and the firmness of the Tories themselves as spurs, Governor Trumbull moved Connecticut toward anti-Tory legislative action on December 14, 1775. Addressing the General Assembly, he called for legislation "to prevent the Operation of the evil practices and designs of persons inimical to the rights and Liberties of the Colonies."[51] The Assembly responded with a comprehensive measure which prohibited providing the British with foodstuffs and military stores, enlisting or encouraging enlistments in the British military, serving with British forces, piloting a British vessel, and even speaking out against the laws of Connecticut or those of the Continental Congress. Persons convicted of giving comfort to the enemy might suffer a loss of all property and imprisonment up to three years. Those who were guilty of criticism of the American cause could be pronounced ineligible for all civil and military offices.[52] By the fall of 1776, with Loyalist sentiment in western Connecticut encouraged by Washington's defeat in New York in September, the Connecticut Assembly hardened its anti-Tory posture. Persons convicted of treason were to be punished by death, and a special committee was established to visit western towns and question "all inimical persons when the ordinary mode of prosecution will not be adequate to the mischief apprehended." Those persons judged "dangerous" by the committee could be detained for as long as the governor and Committee of Safety thought necessary.[53] Armed with comprehensive legislative enactments and justified by the holiness of their cause, Connecticut's Whigs set about completing that purge of conservatives that had begun a decade before with the electoral repudiation of Thomas Fitch.

Most of Connecticut's Loyalists were discovered in the towns west of the Connecticut River.[54] It has been estimated that approximately one-half of them fled to New York to seek the protection of the British. There, many served with the British forces and wound up after the Revolutionary War settling in Nova Scotia and New Brunswick.[55] On the whole, the roughly 1,000 Tories who were either too staunch in their views to flee or else unlucky enough to be identified by the Whigs did not fare as badly in Connecticut as did their counterparts in New York, Pennsylvania, Massachusetts, and Virginia. While the county courts in western Connecticut handled scores of cases during which accused Loyalists were deprived of their property, the courts usually imposed short jail sentences. It appears that there were two factors which accounted for the relative lack of harshness with which Connecticut's Loyalists were treated. First of all, the Tories in western Connecticut were identified and subsequently disarmed fairly early in the Revolutionary War. Those with Loyalist inclinations had no opportunity to offer physical or political opposition in the face of the dominant Whig strength. As a result, there did not take place in Connecticut a protracted Whig-Tory struggle which might have exacerbated the ideological division. Thus, by May, 1777, the General Assembly felt sufficiently secure from a Tory threat to offer pardons to all those who from "ill advice . . . inadvertence and mistaken apprehensions, have absconded and put themselves under the protection of [our] enemies . . . and would probably return to their duty had they assurance of protection. . . ."[56] The evidence indicates that a number of Tories took advantage of this Whig generosity and were able to become reintegrated into Connecticut communities.[57]

The second factor which made less burdensome the plight of Connecticut's Tories was the compassion shown to them by Governor

Trumbull and the Committee of Safety. That Jonathan Trumbull, dominating as always the meetings of the Committee of Safety, should have been responsible for sympathetic treatment of scores of Connecticut Tories was not easily predictable. After all, it was Trumbull who in the crisis of 1774-1775 viewed those in the colony who would not support the Whig position as "depraved, Malignant, avaricious, and haughty." Such a view had inclined Trumbull to sit aside while Tories such as Green and Peters were set upon by Whig mobs. It was also the same Trumbull who, as war governor, hesitated not at all in ordering the imprisonment of those Loyalists who supplied the British with information or provisions,[58] or in approving the confiscation of the property of those Connecticut sons who fought in British regiments.[59] And yet, by 1777, when the state's Tories were disarmed and no longer a threat to Connecticut's security, Jonathan Trumbull's decisions regarding the state's Tories were marked by warm understanding. Trumbull and the Committee of Safety used their pardoning power with consistent compassion. Nine Tories held in Lebanon and Coventry were released upon giving bonds and assurances for their good behavior; six confined in Windham were similarly released; and large numbers held in Stamford and Norwalk likewise were given freedom.[60] A Connecticut Tory physician was given permission to move his family and possessions to the enemy lines.[61] A young Anglican divinity student successfully petitioned Trumbull for permission to journey to London to take holy orders.[62] An Anglican priest, destitute with his church closed, was allowed by Trumbull to relocate in New York,[63] and another Anglican Churchman was given the governor's permission to receive religious tracts from Great Britain.[64] Other Connecticut Tories—ill, destitute, and suffering for having been identified with the Loyalist position—received uniformly kind and sympathetic treatment from the stiff, Lebanon Calvinist.

Similarly kind treatment was accorded by Governor Trumbull and the Committee of Safety to Continental political and military prisoners. Since Washington and the Congress had unshaken confidence in the Whig sentiments of Trumbull and Connecticut, the state was used throughout the Revolutionary War as a depository for prisoners. Trumbull was granted custody of notorious political prisoners such as William Franklin of New Jersey, the Loyalist son of Benjamin Franklin, as well as of British troops who were taken in combat by American forces.[65] Trumbull and the Committee of Saftey distributed the military prisoners in towns such as Litchfield, Farmington, Salisbury, Sharon, Simsbury, Hartford, Wethersfield, and Windham. Trumbull's general inclination was to treat these men in a liberal manner, allowing them the limits of the town and not jailing them.[66] This inclination was, however, shaken when Trumbull heard that the British were deliberately infecting American prisoners of war with smallpox.

However, a soothing letter from Washington convinced the Connecticut governor that the smallpox information was untrue, and Trumbull continued to treat his charges well, always looking forward to their exchange for British-held sons of Connecticut.[67] Of far fore difficulty were the political prisoners such as Franklin. The former New Jersey governor set himself up in his quarters at Middletown and turned out pro-British propaganda. Although his patience was tried, Trumbull did no more than make Franklin's confinement more close.

The same compassion that Jonathan Trumbull demonstrated in his decisions regarding Connecticut's Loyalists and enemy prisoners of war was reflected in the governor's administration of Connecticut's wartime embargo. At the beginning of the war, as we have seen, Trumbull had been successful in encouraging the General Assembly to establish a comprehensive embargo, especially upon Connecticut provisions. While the existence of the embargo up to 1780 did indeed contribute to the state's ability to provision both state and Continental forces, it nevertheless created perplexing decisions for Trumbull and the Committee of Safety. Towns within the state, finding it impossible to survive economically without interstate trade, petitioned Lebanon for special permission to export their produce.[68] More commonly, Trumbull and the committee received requests from state and local authorities in Massachusetts and Rhode Island for the opportunity to purchase badly-needed provisions from Connecticut. Requests came from Plymouth, hit by drought and severe storms, for permission to purchase flour and meat.[69] From Nantucket, the victim of a 1779 storm which destroyed the sheep flocks, came a request to trade fish and rock salt for grain, flour, and meat.[70] Both the governor and the Assembly of Rhode Island requested that Trumbull allow the state to import grain from Connecticut.[71] And, Trumbull, as concerned as any man in the American states with the importance of utilizing all possible resources for the provisioning of Washington's forces, nevertheless demonstrated his sensitivity to human considerations by responding to these calls for assistance by allowing for temporary relaxations of the state's embargo.[72]

Yet, it must be said that Trumbull's handling of the Connecticut Loyalists and prisoners of war, as well as his supervision of the state embargo, revealed more than simply compassionate conduct by the Lebanon governor. Rather, it would appear that in each of these facets of his wartime administration, Trumbull followed that policy which was most likely to enable Connecticut to make a substantial contribution to the Continental cause. While he obviously had no philosophical rapport with Connecticut's Tories, his treatment of them was mild. While his sympathetic posture might have emanated from his understanding of the plight of the state's Loyalists, it might perhaps have stemmed from a realization that harsh actions might simply have contributed to an armed backlash by Connecticut's Tories, a circumstance which only would have complicated the state's military effort. Too, his thoughtful administration of Connecticut's wartime embargo might as well have been a reflection of his desire to encourage as little opposition as possible to the trade limitation which he considered a crucial measure in contributing to Connecticut's ability to provision both state and Continental troops. Trumbull's fear of internal disharmony was certainly revealed in his reaction to a resolution of the General Assembly that the chief state executive officer be addressed as "His Excellency":

> High sounding Titles intoxicate the mind, ingenerate envy, and breed disorders in a Commonwealth, and ought therefore to be avoided. . . . An Act of this Assembly . . . ordered the stile of *His Excellency* to be given the Governor of this State. This savouring too much of High-Titles, and not beneficial, may it not honorably be repealed?[73]

The significance of Trumbull's effective wartime administration cannot be overestimated—it made possible a significant broadening of the prerogatives of the executive in a state in which legislative hegemony was nothing less than a way of life. While the Connecticut General Assembly had made the office of the governor little more than ceremonial, the Assembly sat patiently by during the war years as the former Lebanon merchant in effect unilaterally directed Connecticut's political apparatus.[74] That this executive assertiveness was allowed to be expressed in the state was, of course, no minor element in the contribution which Connecticut was able to make to the achievement of American victory in the Revolutionary War. Indeed, the significance of the executive strength which characterized Connecticut government in the war years can be fully appreciated only by noting the extent to which executive-legislative bickering weakened the war efforts of so many other states during the Revolutionary era.[75]

And yet, for all his success in facilitating the realization of Connecticut's potential during the Revolutionary War, Jonathan Trumbull's last years as governor were troubled by growing popular disaffection. While Trumbull had been such a nearly-unanimous choice for the governorship between 1775 and 1780 that it was popularly held that the General Assembly did not even bother to count the votes, by 1780, Lebanon's first citizen appeared less and less to be the people's choice. In that year's election, apparently for the first time, Trumbull failed to get a majority of the votes cast for the governship. While Trumbull was returned to office by the vote of the General Assembly, 1781 again brought political disappointment. As in the election of 1780, Trumbull once again failed to achieve a majority vote, and once again had his political tenure salvaged by the General Assembly. Although Trumbull seems to have made something of a popular comeback in 1782 by retaining the governorship on the basis of winning a majority of the freemen's votes, by 1783 the elder politico saw his public favor again decline. He failed to secure a majority vote, and the General Assembly once more came to his rescue by electing him governor.

It has been said that Trumbull's political fortunes declined in the early 1780s as a result of a story which circulated through Connecticut to the effect that the war governor had made a fortune by involvement in illicit trade with the British on Long Island. That such a story did make the political rounds was true enough.[76] That it was taken as fact by some was perhaps also true. Throughout the Revolutionary War, a bustling illicit commerce had taken place between the coastal towns in western Connecticut and British-Loyalist communities on Long Island. Although Trumbull and the Committee of Safety in Lebanon had labored energetically to stem this trade by utilizing the efforts of Connecticut Militia, local political authorities in western towns, and special naval patrols,[77] the trade had nevertheless gone on throughout the Revolutionary War. It is possible that the charge against Trumbull originated with persons, who, dissatisfied by the continuation of the illegal trade, concluded that only duplicity by the state's executive rendered Connecticut incapable of terminating the dishonorable traffic with the enemy. Or, perhaps those actually involved in the illicit trade hoped to draw suspicion from western Connecticut by accusing Trumbull of overseeing the clandestine commerce. In any case, Trumbull attempted to squash the slander by calling for an investigation of the charge by the General Assembly in January, 1782.[78] Trumbull was cleared by the subsequent investigation,[79] a circumstance which perhaps accounted for his ability in the election of 1782 to win a popular majority.[80]

Yet, even with the illicit trade charge buried, Trumbull was still confronted by growing public coolness. His 1782 electoral recovery was followed the next year by another instance of his inability to command a popular majority. Clearly, then, Jonathan Trumbull's waning political strength was due to more than the illicit trading charge. Indeed, as one examines Trumbull's predicament in light of the prevailing political winds in Connecticut in the early 1780s, it is evident that the governor from Lebanon began to lose public support because he was associated in the public mind with two conditions which were becoming increasingly distasteful to substantial numbers of the state's freemen—state wartime taxation and national political centralization.

With the exception of the Tory element in the western towns, Connecticut's population had entered the Revolutionary War united on the basis of a Whig-oriented political consensus. But the strains of the war had produced serious internal division in the state, particularly between merchants and farmers. Connecticut's merchants, it would appear, did not fare badly during the Revolution War. Although hurt by the state trade embargo and the British blockade of New England,[81] merchants were able to adjust by exploiting various economic routes. Some state merchants were able to carry on a lucrative trade with the French and Danish possessions in the Caribbean by either securing special permits from Trumbull and the Committee of Safety or by simply ignoring the state embargo.[82] A considerable number of Connecticut merchants became involved in privateering activity which, although fraught with danger, brought spectacular prizes. Some merchants, combining public service with business, had profitable dealings with state and national commissary agents. Finally, a goodly number of western Connecticut merchants appear to have thrown both honor and patriotism to the winds by trading extensively with the British and the Loyalists on Long Island.[83] All in all, then, the mercant community thus had various profitable routes to follow during the war years.

Farmers, on the other hand, found their wartime situation much less encouraging. While some large producers did enjoy the increased demand for their crops and livestock and participated with merchants in the private and public provisions trade, most of Connecticut's small farmers in the northeastern and northwestern sections of the state passed the war years in acute economic distress. Not producing enough of a surplus to become involved in the provisions trade, these farmers were squeezed by the ever-rising prices of manufactured goods. Disturbed by the inability of the state government to establish consistent price regulations, the agrarians complained constantly about the "great pests of society," the merchants who were able to turn wartime scarcity to their own benefit.[84] At the same time, the small farmers were bitter regarding the state's approach to wartime taxation. The agrarians asserted that they had been forced to bear the greatest burden of the new tax bills. Arguing that the wartime taxation measures had established tax rates largely on the basis of real property, the small farmers asserted that they were being crushed by the soaring tax rates, while merchants, many of whose assets were liquid, had generally not been as affected.[85] Although the General Assembly did effect a revision of wartime taxation so that business profits as well as real estate were evaluated as taxable,[86] the small farmers never ceased complaining that they were bearing too large a portion of the increased taxes.[87]

Thus embittered by their experience with wartime taxation, the state's small farmers were extremely sensitive in the closing years of the war toward national political centralization which would have brought with it additional financial burdens. The request of Congress in 1781 for the power to levy an impost of five per cent on goods imported into the United States brought a storm of protest from Connecticut agrarians. Believing that the new impost would be passed on to them in the form of higher prices for the manufactured goods they required, the farmers of northeastern and northwestern Connecticut succeeded through their representatives in the General Assembly in preventing the state from granting the congressional request for the five per cent duty.[88] In addition, Connecticut's small farmers became bitter opponents of the intention of Congress to grant pensions to Revolutionary officers. In the dark days of 1780, when army officers threatened to leave the service in droves because they could not secure payment from Congress, they were encouraged to serve on by a congressional promise to provide them with back pay in full as well as half pay for life.[89] By 1783, when the promises of Congress had still not been matched by action, American officers gathered at Washington's encampment at Newburgh, New York, and demanded an advance on back pay, some provision for the payment of the remainder due, and a settlement of the 1780 promise of half pay for life.[90] Congress was quite willing to grant full back pay, but significant opposition arose over the half pay promise. As a compromise, Congress in March, 1783, agreed to "commute" the half pay for life to full pay for five years after the war.[91] When news of the commutation scheme reached Connecticut, the state's already financially overburdened farmers rose in protest. The representatives in the General Assembly from the northeastern and northwestern farming communities damned commutation as a measure which would create a military aristocracy.[92] The agrarian representatives went on to oppose the plan as an indication of increasing national financial power over the states. The arguments, however, were of little importance. The Connecticut General Assembly, dominated by nationalist-oriented representatives, fought back the farmers' protests and instructed the state delegation in Congress to support commutation.[93]

It is clear, then, that the political consensus with which Connecticut had generally responded to Lexington and Concord was all but shattered by the end of the Revolutionary War. Connecticut's small farmers came to feel themselves ill used by a governmental apparatus which was supportive of the financial interests of surplus-producing farmers and merchants. Disturbed by what they considered to be their oppressive tax burden during the war years, the small farmers came to oppose by the early 1780s any measure which might make their financial situation more difficult. Since Congress, moving in a nationalist direction, was responsible for measures such as the impost and commutation which would ultimately complicate their financial plight, Connecticut's agrarians became foes of any measure or movement which might result in increased power by the national government. Regarding state affairs, Connecticut's small farmers began to single out for their hostility those public figures whose political stance was characterized by support of the state's wartime taxation and of measures which would strengthen national political centralization. What this meant, in effect, was that there would be opposition to the entire wartime political establishment,[94] but most especially, to that figure who personified Connecticut government in the Revolutionary era— Jonathan Trumbull.

Trumbull, of course, had very little in his background or wartime political conduct which the agrarians could praise. Trumbull was, after all, a merchant, one of those "pests" which Connecticut's farmers regarded with uniform disdain. Trumbull's financial antics in the 1760s and 1770s, in addition, could not have endeared him to a farming populace which knew instinctively that a merchant was capable of all sorts of suspicious business gyrations. Even worse than his background, however, was the fact that, as war governor, the Lebanon merchant had taken positions which the farmers of Connecticut detested. Trumbull had been an opponent of that state price regulation which the agrarians had generally sought throughout the war years.[95] While the farmers tended to enjoy wartime inflation as a condition which would make more bearable their debt-ridden situations, the governor had used his influence to prevent Connecticut from excessively utilizing paper money emissions to meet expenses.[96] Perhaps most disturbing to the small farmers, Trumbull had been a consistent champion of increased taxation during the Revolutionary War.[97] It is, therefore, not surprising that by the early 1780s Connecticut's angered agrarian communities were infuriated with the governor from Lebanon and hence motivated to deny him electoral support.

Governor Trumbull could hardly have been unaware of the extent to which his wartime policies were alienating the state's small farmers. Northeastern and northwestern farming communities had been consistent sources of support for price regulation in the General Assembly, in the press, and in town meetings.[98] These same communities had also been responsible for wartime protests in the General Assembly against the state's taxation measures.[99] If Trumbull had any illusions about his probable electoral support from the state's farmers by 1780, they must have been quickly destroyed. The politically astute Jeremiah Wadsworth wrote to Lebanon in March, 1780, that "ambitious and restless spirits . . . are busy to work a change in Government."[100] That which Wadsworth conveyed was promptly confirmed in the election later in the year. Trumbull was denied a popular majority.

On the basis of his usual political *modus operandi*, Trumbull might well have responded to this threat to his political future by adjusting his positions to soothe the ruffled agrarians.

The evidence indicates, however, that Trumbull did no such thing. While he did, as any man unjustly accused would, make certain that the illicit trading charge was unmasked as false, he made no attempt to alter his politics to mollify the aroused agrarians. Rather, he continued on a course that could not but intensify the anger of Connecticut's tax-conscious small farmers.

During the 1781-1782 debate in the General Assembly, when the representatives of the state's northeastern and northwestern farming communities fought to prevent Connecticut approval of the Continental impost, Trumbull made clear that he was an unqualified proponent of the national levy. His speeches were ringing exhortations to provide the national government with financial strength.[101] Trumbull reinforced his nationalistic posture during the state debate over commutation in 1783. While the agrarian element raged in the General Assembly and in the press against commutation, Trumbull offered support for the measure. He maintained that for the United States not to meet its promises to the Revolutionary officers would constitute nothing less than a breach of national responsibility. Against the provincial, antinationalistic assertions of the agrarians, the governor held in a speech to the General Assembly in May, 1783, that Congress must be given the power and financial support to meet its national responsibilities. He emphasized that all who had financial claims upon the United States "should be treated with justice, and for that end provision made to pay the annual interest on the sums . . . due."[102]

It would appear, then, that during these debates in the early 1780s, Jonathan Trumbull made known his convictions with uncharacteristic boldness. He took a line and followed it with vigor, despite the fact that his action would undoubtedly harm his public career. Indeed, his nationalistic support of the Continental impost and commutation was certainly the decisive element in his inability to command a popular majority in the elections of 1781 and 1783.[103]

Jonathan Trumbull's decision in the early 1780s to endanger his political future on behalf of the strengthening of the financial power of Congress was but another reflection of his total absorption in the cause of American nationhood. Convinced that the cause of America was synonymous with that of the Lord, the Lebanon Puritan, as he had since the Stamp Act crisis, clearly had found a public issue the resolution of which caused him to deny personal considerations.

Still, despite the intensity of his desire to foster national strength, Trumbull by 1783 was ready to call an end to his public career. While it is not improbable that the growing opposition to his governorship contributed to his decision to retire, it is more likely that the Lebanon politician made up his mind to retire because he was exhausted by the wartime labors. Coming to the Connecticut governorship in 1769 at age 59, Trumbull, by 1783, had borne the burdens of the office for fourteen brutally-demanding years. He had endured what must have been nerve-wracking anxiety in the first half of the 1770s when America and Britain were moving toward physical confrontation. Even more of a strain was the labor of the war years. Charged with wide-ranging responsibilities that exceeded those of any Connecticut chief executive before or after the Revolutionary War, Trumbull daily had to make decisions with his Committee of Safety that went to the root of the state's war effort. That the man was able to stand up to the never-ending demands of the war governorship was incredible testament to the rigor of his Puritan constitution.

In short, then, it is not difficult to see that by 1783 Governor Jonathan Trumbull, having borne endless public and personal trials during the war years, was quite ready for retirement. While there is no reference to illness in his correspondence, the fact that he was to die by the summer of 1785 leads one to conclude that he must have been experiencing signs of physical decline by the time he decided to retire. Still, worn out as he must have been by his wartime burdens, Trumbull possessed sufficient strength of body and will to make his farewell speech to the Connecticut General Assembly a medium for the expression of that nationalistic conviction to which he was so firmly attached. Appearing before the Assembly in October, 1783, Trumbull made it clear that his retirement, which was to be effected when his term expired in May, 1784, did not signify any diminution of his ardent nationalistic posture:

> The existence of a Congress, vested with powers competent to the great national purposes for which that body was instituted, is essential to our national security, establishment, and independence. Whether Congress is already vested with such powers, is a question, worthy, in my opinion, of the most serious, candid, and dispassionate consideration of this legislature. . . . For my own part, I do not hesitate to pronounce that, in my opinion, that body is not possessed of those powers which are absolutely necessary to the best management and direction of the general weal, or the fulfilment of our own expectations. This defect in our federal constitution I have already lamented as the cause of many inconveniences which we have experienced; and unless wisely remedied, will, I forsee, be productive of evils, disaterous, if not fatal to our future union and confederation.[104]

Trumbull could not have been heartened by the General Assembly's reaction to his speech. While the nationalist-oriented council voted Trumbull thanks for his distinguished services to the state and resolved to endorse the political sentiments which were expressed in the speech, the House of Representatives, influenced by the agrarian element, demanded that there be no endorsement of Trumbull's nationalist sentiments. The conflict was resolved at a conference attended by members of the council and the house. The views of the representatives of the lower house prevailed, and the formal General Assembly response to the Trumbull speech was a gracious celebration of the retiring governor's state service which made no reference to Trumbull's nationalist admonitions.[105] Trumbull must have thought that he had lost in this confrontation with the anti-nationalist agrarians. He would have been elated, however, had he known that the agrarians, although victorious in this battle, were about to lose the war.

There took place in Connecticut in late 1783 and early 1784 a concerted push to foster nationalist sentiment in the state. It appears that mercantile and large-farming elements became disturbed by the growing political influence of the anti-nationalist agrarians. The Middletown Convention in September, 1783, as well as the agrarian-dominated Assembly's response to Trumbull's speech, left no doubt that the agrarian element intended to continue agitation against the Connecticut political establishment in order to prevent any further state support for national political centralization.

Aroused to this threat to its continuing political tenure, Connecticut's Standing Order struck back. Oliver Ellsworth, Samuel Huntington, Benjamin Huntington, Roger Sherman, Richard Law, Abraham Davenport, Eliphalet Dyer, and Oliver Wolcott set in motion a political crusade aimed at holding off the agrarians in the election of 1784. The state's principal newspaper, the *Connecticut Courant*, clearly reflected its association with the establishment in the winter and spring by publishing piece after piece which maintained that the electoral success of the Middletown anti-nationalist slate would be a prelude to the emergence of anarchy in Connecticut. Trumbull's October, 1783, speech was not only run in the *Courant*, but also distributed widely throughout the state. While the agrarians were highly motivated, it appears that they were no match for the aroused establishment. Having to confront the state's political veterans, as well as the Connecticut tradition of electoral support for the existing political order, was too much of a challenge for the determined agrarians. As they would be during Connecticut's debate over the ratification of the Constitution in 1788, the agrarians were swamped in the election of 1784.

The nationalists captured the governorship with the election of Matthew Griswold [106] and won majority strength in both houses of the legislature.[107] The significance of the election of 1784 was promptly demonstrated. The newly-formed, nationalist-oriented General Assembly approved the Continental impost, the measure which the agrarians had been fighting since 1781.[108] A few days later, on May 21, 1784, the General Assembly provided Jonathan Trumbull with a glittering farewell. The governor was presented with a warm and glowing memorial of gratitude:[109]

> Sir, Your having conducted us, under the smiles of a propitious Providence, through a long, perilous, and bloody war, to the wished-for haven of rest, Independence, and peace, having completed the circle of public duty marked out to you by heaven, and being wearied with the fatigues of a long and arduous administration, in an advanced age, have voluntarily taken your leave of public service and employment, and are now about to retire to the peaceful walks of private life.
>
> Permit us, Sir, the Representative of a grateful people, to assure you that in your retirement from public service, we shall entertain the most

lively sense of your eminent services and distinguished merit—and that our fervent prayer is that the Almighty would take you into his holy keeping, make the residue of your days many and happy as your services have been long, prolong to mankind the blessing of your wise consels and great example, and make your exit out of time, whenever it may happen, trumphant and peaceful, and your immorality glorious.

The public career of Jonathan Trumbull then ended as he was escorted out of Hartford toward Lebanon by members of the General Assembly, officers of the Connecticut Militia, and the splendidly-garbed horsemen of the Governor's Guard.[110]

Retirement

J ONATHAN TRUMBULL's last years must have seemed strangely quiet to a man whose life had been solely consecrated to the performance of mercantile and public responsibilities. Even though Trumbull's duties in the public service were not terminated until his retirement in May, 1784, his workload as Connecticut's governor began to decrease in 1782-83 as the Revolutionary War was drawing to a close. At the same time, Trumbull made the decision not to resume his mercantile activity. He received invitations from Hamburg, Haiti, and Amsterdam to establish trading operations,[1] but the state of his health must have convinced him that his constitution was not sufficiently strong to bear the strains of mercantile activity.

There were, however, certain responsibilities still to be met. His last years were clouded, as indeed was so much of his life, by his outstanding debts. In April, 1783, Trumbull wrote similar letters to his two principal London creditors. He told both that with the resumption of peace he hoped to deal with his creditors. His pronounced intention, as always, was far removed from what he was actually prepared to do. Not having a chance in the world of actually paying the almost £15,000 that he then owed, Trumbull resorted to the same delaying tactics that he had used so effectively in the late 1760s and 1770s. He told his London creditors that his money was invested in "the public funds of this country," and if the securities were acceptable, he would meet his responsibilities by turning them over to the British firms.[2]

If the London traders had explored the validity of Trumbull's assertion, they would undoubtedly have found that the Connecticut governor had little if any funds invested in such securities. However, as Trumbull must have well known, London traders were not likely to accept American securities which were at best of dubious value, considering the state of Continental finances. One of his London creditors, probably long since resigned to writing off the Lebanon merchant as a bad job, simply turned over his account to an attorney.[3] The other, Lane, Son, and Fraser, declined the offer of the securities, choosing to retain the Trumbull mortgages instead.[4]

By February, 1785, Lane, Son, and Fraser informed Trumbull that his mortgages were transferred to Boston attorneys who would sell the property.[5] Trumbull responded to this pressure by reducing his indebtedness in the spring of 1785. The General Assembly voted Trumbull £3,000 for salary arrears and expense money in May, 1785, and it appears that a small portion of the sum was transferred to his creditors.[6] Nevertheless, when Trumbull died in August, 1785, he had outstanding debts amounting to over £14,000 and assets totaling only £6,800.[7] The assertion by one of Trumbull's biographers that Trumbull's sons paid even a part of the debt is very doubtfull indeed.[9] It is considerably more likely that Trumbull's creditors never received justice, in spite of the patience and understanding with which they had always dealt with the Lebanon merchant.

In his last years, Trumbull returned to the scholarly interests of his youth. As in the days when he was preparing to assume the pulpit in Colchester, he wrote sermons, copies of which he sent to President Stiles of Yale.[10] He returned once again to the study of Hebrew which he had begun so long ago at Harvard.[11] Yet, such diversions left Jonathan Trumbull for the first time in his activity-filled mature years with time to himself. He must have sat frequently before a roaring fire in his quiet house in Lebanon. His daily walks must have taken him often to the Lebanon cemetery where he stood beside the graves of Joseph, Faith, and his wife. As he mused over the scenes of his life, the aged man perhaps experienced varying emotions.

Certainly the contemplation of his business career must have struck the man with frustration and shame. As he mulled over the lost opportunities and the fruitless plans, he could not have felt anything but exasperation at how all had come to humiliating failure. A man of Trumbull's vanity must have been constantly maddened by the degree to which his business failure made him an object of public derision. Perhaps his natural inclination to labor was reinforced during the war years by a desire to cleanse himself of the frustration which his business collapse had caused him. Too, Trumbull must have experienced shame at the deceitful tactics he had used to hold off his creditors. No man brought up according to the struct Puritan code by which Trumbull had been reared could have been so adept at rationalization as to justify to himself tactics based upon deception. And, it must be said, there was deception indeed in Trumbull's conduct. By the late 1760s and early 1770s it was obvious that there was no way by which

Trumbull could have reversed his business fortunes and paid his creditors. Further, his conduct at the end of the war was but a continuation of his tried and true stalling tactics, a fact which no amount of rationalization could hide. Perhaps Trumbull was able to take some comfort from the thought that he had refused the honorable course of declaring bankruptcy in order to protect his family. Still, there must have been pain when Jonathan Trumbull considered all this, pain which must have made the old man's steps a little slower and his failing body a little less erect.

And yet, if musings of his business career brought pain to Trumbull, he must have glowed with satisfaction as he contemplated his public career. Probably finding it easy to view his cautious political conduct from the 1730s to the 1770s as having been necessary to enable him to be in a position to assume the governorship during the turbulent Revolutionary era, Trumbull could have taken justifiable pride in his service as Connecticut governor during the Revolutionary War. He had performed his wartime duties with an energy and a thoughtfulness matched by few contemporary political leaders. His herculean labors and logistical skills had been in great measure responsible for that successful state mobilization which had made possible Connecticut's magnificent contribution to the American cause. While other states were weakened by internal friction and disharmonies, Trumbull's thoughtful administration of the state's domestic affairs had kept Connecticut's internal difficulties to a minimum. And, when the prolonged sacrifices of the war had produced manifestations of provincialism among Connecticut's small farmers, Trumbull had been quite willing to risk his own political future in order to support that national political centralization without which the emerging American nation could not have long survived.

That Trumbull's wartime services had won him respect and admiration on both sides of the Atlantic was a fact beyond dispute. In 1779, Yale College had conferred upon Trumbull the honorary degree of Doctor of Civil Law.[12] At the close of the war, the University of Edinburgh granted Trumbull an LL.D., [13] and Trumbull was informed by President Stiles of Yale that he had been elected to the American Academy of Arts and Sciences.[14] Political tributes to Trumbull came from various quarters. At the conclusion of the war, Eliphalet Dyer had written from Philadelphia, where he was a member of the Connecticut delegation to Congress:

> I heartily rejoice, Sir, that in the laborious part you have taken in your advanced years, in the important station which Providence has assigned you, in which, with unwearied application, you have exerted your utmost abilities, with patience, hope, and perservance, in the cause and service of your country, and in the greatest trials and darkest hours of our conflict, with a firm and unshaken reliance on Divine Providence,

that God has supported and continued your valuable life at length to see the joyful day of her Deliverance.[15]

The Continental Congress, via Robert Livingston, sent Trumbull congratulations on the achievement of American independence: "This event of divine Providence is truly marvelous in our eyes, and demands our highest gratitude and praise to Almighty God. It relieves us from the distresses of war, and affords the fairest prospect of the future happiness and prosperity of the United States of America. I do most sincerely congratulate you on this great event."[16] At the same time, Ezra Stiles, in the course of an address to the Connecticut General Assembly, had said to the governor that the state's freemen "account ourselves happy that, by the free election and annual voice of citizens, God hath for so many years past called you up to the supreme Magistracy in this commonwealth."[17] Similar testimonials had come to Trumbull earlier from the Frenchmen, Rochambeau and Luzerne.[18]

While these honors had undoubtedly contributed to the sense of pride which Trumbull must have experienced as he thought of his public career, it was perhaps true that no recognition that Trumbull achieved was as satisfying to him as the knowledge that his wartime efforts had won him the respect and friendship of George Washington. That the urbane Virginian and the Connecticut Puritan should have become respectful and warm friends might at first glance seem strange. Yet, the two were clearly joined by their absolute determination to foster the emergence of a strong, united American nation.

Washington came to realize during the war that Trumbull was always to be counted upon in an emergency, that he had the vision to eschew personal and local considerations, and that, despite all complications, he would under all circumstances leave no effort untended in contributing to American victory. For Trumbull's part, he saw in Washington an olympian figure, who, in the face of military reverses, public indifference, political friction, and fiscal confusion, by the strength of his character alone kept the struggling army in the field until victory was achieved. Their wartime correspondence reveals that they were intimate confidants who shared personal and public joys and distresses,[19] and, by the end of the war, they held each other in unreserved esteem. Addressing Washington in June, 1783, in the name of the citizens of Connecticut, Trumbull wrote:

Permit me . . . to assure you how great pleasure and satisfaction we have enjoyed, in the wisdom, magnanimity, and skill shown in forming, disciplining, and conducting the army of the United States . . . and also in the patriotic virtue . . . which exhibits the foundation principles so necessary . . . to maintain and support an indissoluble union of the States, under one federal head, a sacred regard to public justice, a proper peace establishment, and a pacific and friendly disposition among the people of the United States.[20]

Upon receiving from Trumbull, Jr., a copy of the address which Governor Trumbull delivered to the General Assembly in October, 1783, Washington wrote to his former secretary:

> The sentiments contained in it are such as would do honor to a patriot of any age or Nation; at least, they are too coincident with my own, not to meet with my warmest approbation. Be so good as to present my most cordial respects to the Governor and let him know that it is my wish, the mutual friendship and esteem which have been planted and fostered in the tumult of public life, may not wither and die in the serenity of retirement: tell him we should rather amuse our evening hours of Life in cultivating the tender plants, and bringing them to perfection, before they are transplanted to a happier clime.[21]

And, a short time later, Washington wrote directly to Trumbull:

> Believe me, my dear Sir, there is no disparity in our ways of thinking and acting. . . . No correspondence can be more pleasing than one which originates from similar sentiments, and similar Conduct through . . . a painful contest. I pray you therefore to continue me among the number of your friends, and to favor me with such observations as shall occur.

Jonathan Trumbull could indeed have warmed himself in his last years with the knowledge that he had won the plaudits of his contemporaries—from Washington to the Connecticut freemen who vindicated the retiring governor's nationalist sentiments in the election of 1784.[23] As much satisfaction as Trumbull derived from these kudos, as much perhaps as they might have helped to cancel the man's frustration over his mercantile failure, it is probably true that if Trumbull in his last days on earth had a sense of his fulfillment as a man, that sense did not emanate from the esteem of his contemporaries. Rather, it came from Trumbull's conviction that his service to his country had been in the name of the Lord. Trumbull had seen the Revolutionary War as a battle to preserve the purity of America, as a conflict to insure that his land, this "City upon a Hill," would remain as proof to all mankind that a society constructed on the basis of God's Word could endure and prosper. He viewed his own efforts in the struggle as well as the ultimate success of the cause as having been the will of God. He wrote to Henry Laurens in October, 1783: "That Superintendent of Wisdom which governs human Affairs has brought to a happy Termination our arduous Contest. It has brought these United States to be named among the Nations of the Earth as a free, independent and Sovereign People. . . . Suffer me to congratulate you on this great Event—an Event . . .undoubtedly in the Works of Heaven, one as such claims our utmost Gratitude and Love to the Disposer of all Events."[24] If, then, it is true that Jonathan Trumbull's death on August 17, 1785, after a short illness, came to a man who appeared to be "waiting for the Lord—and when death came was . . . blessed,"[25] it was so because the dying man was at peace, knowing that he had kept his Covenant with the Puritan God who had charged his children to make America "a beacon for all mankind."

Notes

THE MAKING OF THE MAN

1. The early family history of the Trumbulls is noted in I. W. Stuart, *Life of Jonathan Trumbull* (Boston, 1859), pp. 25-26; Jonathan Trumbull, *Jonathan Trumbull: Governor of Connecticut, 1769-1784* (Boston, 1919), pp. 1-3; and Glenn Weaver, *Jonathan Trumbull: Connecticut's Merchant Magistrate* (Hartford, 1956), p. 3.

2. Theodore Sizer, ed., *The Autobiography of Colonel John Trumbull: Patriot-Artist, 1756-1843* (New Haven, 1953), p. 2.

3. Weaver, *Jonathan Trumbull*, pp. 5-6.

4. J. H. Trumbull and C. J. Hoadly, compilers, *The Public Records of the Colony of Connecticut* (15 vols.: Hartford, 1850-1890), VI, 59; VII, 154; and VII, 298. Hereinafter cited as *Connecticut Colonial Records*.

5. Albert E. Van Dusen, *Connecticut* (New York, 1961), p. 109.

6. François J. DeChastellux, *Travels in North America* (2 vols.: London, 1787), I, 33.

7. The oft-cited Winthrop sermon is reprinted in Perry Miller, ed., *The American Puritans: Their Prose and Poetry* (New York, 1956), pp. 79-84.

8. Perry Miller and Thomas H. Johnson, eds., *The Puritans* (2 vols.: New York, 1938), I, 60-61.

9. Richard L. Bushman, *From Puritan to Yankee: Character and Social Order in Connecticut, 1690-1765* (Cambridge, 1967), pp. 3-21.

10. Bernard Bailyn, *The New England Merchants in the Seventeenth Century* (Cambridge, 1955), pp. 16, 20-23.

11. Stuart, *Life of Jonathan Trumbull*, pp. 28-29.

12. Weaver, *Jonathan Trumbull*, p. 7.

LEBANON MERCHANT

1. Weaver, *Jonathan Trumbull*, pp. 13ff. gives Trumbull's mercantile career in detail.

2. *Connecticut Colonial Records*, VII, 424.

3. *Ibid.*, VIII, 27.

4. *Ibid.*, VIII, 4, 281.

5. *Ibid.*, VIII, 159.

6. Bushman, *From Puritan to Yankee*, pp. 10-11.

7. Weaver, *Jonathan Trumbull*, p. 27.

8. Hartford *Courant*, June 13, 1780.

9. Quoted in Clifford K. Shipton, "Jonathan Trumbull," *Sibley's Harvard Graduates: Biographical Sketches of Those Who Attended Harvard College* (Boston, 1951), VIII, 269.

10. Weaver, *Jonathan Trumbull*, p. 20.

11. Margaret E. Martin, *Merchants and Trade of the Connecticut River Valley, 1750-1820* (Northampton, Massachusetts, 1929), pp. 41, 144-145, 156-161.

12. Weaver, *Jonathan Trumbull*, pp. 18-20.

13. *Ibid.*, p. 19.

14. *Ibid.*, pp. 25-29, 99-100.

15. Jackson Turner Main, *The Social Structure of Revolutionary America* (Princeton, New Jersey, 1965), although concentrating on the period 1763-1788, notes that attitudes he describes preceded the Revolutionary era. See especially pp. 207-208.

16. Weaver, *Jonathan Trumbull*, pp. 20-21, 90.

17. *Connecticut Colonial Records*, IX, 211-212.

18. Weaver, *Jonathan Trumbull*, pp. 41-79.

19. *Connecticut Colonial Records*, X, 481-483; XI, 480-487.

20. Weaver, *Jonathan Trumbull*, pp. 27-28, 72. Martha Williams Hooker, "Booklovers of 1783—One of the First Libraries in America," *Connecticut Magazine*, X (December, 1906), 715-723.

21. Sizer, ed., *The Autobiography of Colonel John Trumbull*, p. 4.

22. *Connecticut Colonial Records*, VIII, 26, 53, 119, 156, 189, 222, 258, 286, 365, 446, 512; IX, 3, 103, 188, 268, 350, 415, 501; X, 243, 354, 489; XI, 3, 116, 246, 368, 494.

23. *Ibid.*, IX, 88, 234; X, 448-449, 593; XI, 100-108.

24. *Ibid.*, IX, 6, 104, 189, 271, 351, 425, 502, 505; X, 4, 71, 153, 154, 245, 356, 490; XI, 4, 5, 117, 118, 247, 372, 496, 499.

25. *Ibid.*, X, 1.

26. *Ibid.*, X, 198.

27. In explaining Trumbull's mercantile decline, it must be noted that the Lebanon merchant's business was hurt by a series of serious losses at sea, especially in the 1760s. Too, he had ignored the sound advice in the 1750s of Samuel Sparrow who advised that Trumbull produce pearl-ash for sale in Britain. Trumbull, rather, explored such will-o-the-wisps as Nantucket oil and Connecticut masts. Finally, one must recognize that conditions indigenous to the situation of an American merchant had detracted from the possibility of Trumbull's success. The dearth of specie in colonial America undoubtedly contributed to his plight, as well as did the currency fluctuations in New England during his active mercantile years. Yet, in the last analysis, merchants faced with comparable complications managed to achieve substantial success. Thus, one must conclude that Trumbull himself, with his foolish credit policy, was the architect of his windblown business house. See David M. Roth, "Jonathan Trumbull, 1710-1785: Connecticut's Puritan Patriot" (Unpublished Dissertation, Clark University, 1971), pp. 70-73.

28. See the mercantile correspondence in the Jonathan Trumbull, Sr., Papers, The Connecticut Historical Society, Box III.

29. See Roth, *op. cit.*, pp. 104-113.

30. *Ibid.*, pp. 115-124.

POLITICAL APPRENTICESHIP, 1736-1763

1. Oscar Zeichner, *Connecticut's Years of Controversy, 1750-1776* (Chapel Hill, North Carolina, 1949), pp. 9-10.

2. Bushman, *From Puritan to Yankee*, pp. 3-21.

3. *Connecticut Colonial Records*, VIII, 22.

4. Zeichner, *Connecticut's Years of Controversy*, pp. 3-5.

5. *Ibid.*, p. 11.

6. *Ibid.*, pp. 29-30.

7. Bushman, *From Puritan to Yankee*, pp. 73-82.

8. *Ibid.*, pp. 164-182.

9. Van Dusen, *Connecticut*, pp. 117-119.

10. Van Dusen, *Connecticut*, pp. 117-119; Zeichner, *Connecticut's Years of Controversy*, pp. 21-27; Bushman, *From Puritan to Yankee*, pp. 183-232.

11. *Connecticut Colonial Records*, VIII, 175, 212, 242, 245-246, 343-354; IX, 134, 380, 428, 445, 467, 538-539, 566-567; X, 219-220; XI, 412, 460, 559.

12. Van Dusen, *Connecticut*, pp. 93-94.

13. Clarence W. Bowen, *The Boundary Disputes of Connecticut* (Boston, 1882), pp. 60-61.

14. *Connecticut Colonial Records*, IX, 301, 339-340.

15. *Ibid.*, IX, 431-433.

16. *Ibid.*, IX, 547-548.

17. Van Dusen, *Connecticut*, p. 94.

18. *Connecticut Colonial Records*, IX, 83-89, 93-99; Van Dusen, *Connecticut*, p. 100; and George A. Wood, *William Shirley, Governor of Massachusetts, 1741-1756* (New York, 1920), pp. 220-287.

19. *Connecticut Colonial Records*, IX, 214; Shipton, "Jonathan Trumbull," *loc. cit.*, pp. 272-273.

20. *Connecticut Colonial Records*, X, 420.

21. *Ibid.*, X, 442-443.

22. *Ibid.*, X, 458.

23. *Ibid.*, X, 593-594.

24. *Ibid.*, X, 598-599.

25. *Ibid.*, XI, 63-64.

26. *Ibid.*, XI, 104.

27. Van Dusen, *Connecticut*, p. 103; "Rolls of Connecticut Men in the French and Indian War," II, *Connecticut Historical Society Collections* (Hartford, 1905), X, 99-178; Lawrence H. Gipson, *The British Empire Before the American Revolution* (15 vols.: New York, 1936-1970), VII, 349-356, 360-427.

28. Roland Mather Hooker, *The Spanish Ship Case: A Troublesome Episode for Connecticut, 1752-1758*, Tercentenary Commission of the State of Connecticut, *Pamphlet* Number 35 (New Haven, 1934), pp. 1, 24. The Hooker pamphlet, probably the most comprehensive survey of the episode, is the basis for the discussion herein.

29. *Ibid.*, p. 28.

30. *Connecticut Colonial Records*, X, 486.

31. Hooker, *The Spanish Ship Case*, pp. 29-30.

32. *Ibid.*, pp. 31-33.

33. *Connecticut Colonial Records*, VIII, 372, 353-354, 515-516; IX, 7, 106, 272, 329-330, 418; X, 7, 96, 286, 389.

34. Trumbull served on committees which dealt with the colony's expenses in the Cape Breton expedition (1745), the expedition against Canada (1747), the attack against Crown Point (1756), and the attack on Fort William Henry (1758). *Connecticut Colonial Records*, IX, 88, 294; X, 461; XI, 127.

35. *Connecticut Colonial Records*, VIII, 421-422, 519; IX, 36-37, 290-291, 454; X, 131-132.

36. *Ibid.*, X, 288.

37. Zeichner, *Connecticut's Years of Controversy*, p. 27.

38. Shipton, "Jonathan Trumbull," *loc. cit.*, pp. 271, 272.

39. Trumbull, *Jonathan Trumbull*, pp. 58-59.

40. *Ibid.*, p. 59.

41. Weaver, *Jonathan Trumbull*, p. 75.

1. See Zeichner, *Connecticut's Years of Controversy*, pp. 46-50.

2. *Ibid.*, pp. 20-43, 50-52.

3. *Ibid.*, pp. 56-57.

4. One thinks in this context of Trumbull's former partner, Colonel Fitch of Windham. As the imperial crisis deepened, Fitch spoke out in Windham against the physical pressure that was applied to moderates by Patriot radicals. Fitch shortly found himself subject to social isolation and an economic boycott. See Zeichner, *Connecticut's Years of Controversy*, pp. 174, 231.

5. See Bushman, *From Puritan to Yankee*, pp. 135-143.

6. Edmund S. Morgan, "The Puritan Ethic and the American Revolution," *William and Mary Quarterly*, Third Series, XXIV (January, 1967), p. 16.

7. A principal source of information on British politics in the 1760s is the correspondence to the Connecticut government of William Samuel Johnson who was sent to Britain to represent the colony in its land dispute of the period with the Mohegan Indians. Johnson's letters to Connecticut, available to Trumbull as deputy governor (1766-1769), noted in detail the corruption and inattention to public business which he observed in British government. See the Trumbull Papers, *Massachusetts Historical Society Collections*, Fifth Series, IX (1885), 213-483.

8. *Ibid.*, IX, 270-275. Johnson to William Pitkin, April 29, 1768.

9. *Ibid.*, IX, 239-252. Johnson to William Pitkin, July 13, 1767.

10. *Ibid.*, IX, 264-269. Johnson to William Pitkin, March 12, 1768.

11. *Fitch Papers, Connecticut Historical Society Collections* (2 vols.: Hartford, 1918-1920), II, 355.

12. Trumbull to William Samuel Johnson, June 23, 1767. Quoted in Shipton, "Jonathan Trumbull," *loc. cit.*, p. 278.

13. Trumbull to Richard Jackson, April 25, 1768. Quoted in Shipton, "Jonathan Trumbull," *loc. cit.*, p. 278. Jackson was a member of Parliament who served in the period as Connecticut's agent.

14. Ellen D. Larned, *History of Windham County* (2 vols.: Worcester, Massachusetts, 1874-1880), II, 102-103, noted one of Trumbull's decisions in which he took a liberal stand regarding a tax exemption for Baptists.

15. Shipton, "Jonathan Trumbull," *loc. cit.*, p. 279; Zeichner, *Connecticut's Years of Controversy*, p. 143.

16. Jonathan Trumbull to William Samuel Johnson, June 23, 1767, William Samuel Johnson Papers, The Connecticut Historical Society.

17. Quoted in Zeichner, *Connecticut's Years of Controversy*, p. 84.

18. Although successful in the election of 1770, Trumbull had a somewhat embarrassing time when the moderates backing Fitch had an opportunity to focus on the financial problems of the radical candidate for the governorship. A popular ditty of the campaign began with the line: "Now Will [Pitkin] is dead and his Purser [Trumbull] broke." See Zeichner, *Connecticut's Years of Controversy*, pp. 123-124. The radical forces were able, however, to overcome this assault on Trumbull by maintaining that Connecticut would be in the hands of a man who was "favourable to parliamentary encroachments" if Fitch were returned to office. Nevertheless, in every election for the next thirteen years Trumbull's foes always revived for the electorate the image of the "broke" governor.

19. Zeichner, *Connecticut's Years of Controversy*, p. 28.

20. *Ibid.*, p. 97.

21. *Ibid.*, pp. 97-98.

22. *Ibid.*, p. 98. Van Dusen, *Connecticut*, p. 120; and Origen S. Seymour, *The Beginnings of the Episcopal Church in Connecticut*, Tercentenary Commission

of the State of Connecticut, *Pamphlet* Number 30 (New Haven, 1934), pp. 1-5.

23. Jonathan Trumbull to William Samuel Johnson, December 12, 1769, Trumbull Papers, *Massachusetts Historical Society Collections,* Fifth Series, IX (1885), 388-391.

24. William Samuel Johnson to Jonathan Trumbull, February 26, 1770, *Ibid.,* 411-418.

25. Zeichner, *Connecticut's Years of Controversy,* p. 32.

26. Albert Laverne Olson, *Agricultural Economy and the Population in Eighteenth-Century Connecticut,* Tercentenary Commission of the State of Connecticut, *Pamphlet* Number 40 (New Haven, 1935), pp. 10-11.

27. *Ibid.,* p. 11; Zeichner, *Connecticut's Years of Controversy,* p. 144.

28. *Connecticut Colonial Records,* XIII, 427-428.

29. *Ibid.,* XIII, 427-428; Zeichner, *Connecticut's Years of Controversy,* p. 145.

30. The Jonathan Trumbull Papers, Connecticut State Library, XX, 72cd.

31. Zeichner, *Connecticut's Years of Controversy,* p. 146.

32. *Connecticut Colonial Records,* XIV, 217-219.

33. Zeichner, *Connecticut's Years of Controversy,* pp. 159-162.

34. *Ibid.,* p. 163.

35. *Ibid.,* pp. 163-165.

36. *Ibid.,* pp. 171-172.

37. The Jonathan Trumbull Papers, Connecticut State Library, IV, Part 1, 13-14.

38. Zeichner, *Connecticut's Years of Controversy,* pp. 92, 175.

39. *Ibid.,* p. 175.

40. See Samuel Peters, "History of Jonathan Trumbull . . .," *loc. cit.,* 6-10; and the Samuel Peters Papers at the New York Historical Society.

41. Shipton, "Jonathan Trumbull," *loc. cit.,* p. 280.

42. Jonathan Trumbull to J. Phelps, September 8, 1774, and Jonathan Trumbull to Joseph Spencer, September 22, 1774, The Jonathan Trumbull Papers, Connecticut State Library, XX, Part I, 89d, 90.

43. Quoted in Shipton, "Jonathan Trumbull," *loc. cit.,* p. 281.

44. *Ibid.,* p. 281.

45. Zeichner, *Connecticut's Years of Controversy,* p. 183.

46. The Jonathan Trumbull Papers, Connecticut State Library, XX, Part I, 101a-101c.

47. *Connecticut Colonial Records,* XIV, 381-393.

48. Shipton, "Jonathan Trumbull," *loc. cit.,* p. 282.

WAR GOVERNOR: CONTINENTAL AFFAIRS

1. Weaver, *Jonathan Trumbull,* p. 150.

2. Malone, ed., *Dictionary of American Biography,* IX, 416.

3. *Ibid.,* IX, 416.

4. *Ibid.,* IX, 416.

5. *Ibid.,* IX, 416-417.

6. *Ibid.,* IX, 417.

7. Jonathan Trumbull to Joseph Trumbull, October 2, 1775, Jonathan Trumbull, Sr., Papers, The Connecticut Historical Society, Box III.

8. Stuart, *Life of Jonathan Trumbull,* p. 195.

9. Theodore Sizer, ed., *The Autobiography of Colonel John Trumbull . . .,* p. 21.

10. Trumbull, *Jonathan Trumbull,* pp. 175-176.

11. Malone, ed., *Dictionary of American Biography,* XIX, 18-19.

12. Victor L. Johnson, *The Administration of the American Commissariat During the Revolutionary War* (Philadelphia, 1941), p. 5.

13. *Ibid.*, p. 26.

14. Shortly after the British withdrew from Boston in March, 1776, Washington evaluated Joseph Trumbull's efforts in supplying the American troops: "Few Armies, if any, have been better and more plentifully supplied than the Troops under Mr. Trumbull's care." George Washington to the President of Congress, June 28, 1776. John C. Fitzpatrick, ed., *The Writings of George Washington* (39 vols.: Washington, D.C., 1933-1944), V, 192.

15. Johnson, *The American Commissariat*, pp. 38-40, 42, 43, 45-50, 53-56, 62, and 65.

16. *Ibid.*, pp. 122-125.

17. *Ibid.*, p. 75.

18. Jonathan Trumbull, "Joseph Trumbull, The First Commissary-General of the Continental Army," *Records and Papers of the New London County Historical Society*, Part III, Volume II (1897), p. 346.

19. Joseph Trumbull to James Bates, February 23, 1778; Eliphalet Dyer to Joseph Trumbull, July 8, 1778, Joseph Trumbull Papers, The Connecticut Historical Society, Box IV.

20. Jonathan Trumbull to Jonathan Trumbull, Jr., July 6, 1778; Jonathan Trumbull to General Horatio Gates, August 18, 1778, Jonathan Trumbull, Sr., Papers, The Connecticut Historical Society, Box IV.

21. Stuart, *Life of Jonathan Trumbull*, p. 510.

22. *Connecticut Courant*, June 13, 1780.

23. Stuart, *Life of Jonathan Trumbull*, pp. 513-514.

24. *Connecticut Courant*, June 13, 1780; Stuart, *Life of Jonathan Trumbull*, p. 513.

25. See, for example, Jonathan Trumbull to David Trumbull, August 14, 1777; Jonathan Trumbull to Jonathan Trumbull, Jr., July 6, 1778, Jonathan Trumbull, Sr., Papers, The Connecticut Historical Society, Box IV.

26. John served at Dorchester Heights (1776), at Crown Point and Ticonderoga (1777), in Pennsylvania (1778), and in Rhode Island (1777 and 1778). See Sizer, ed., *The Autobiography of Colonel John Trumbull . . .*, pp. 17, 22-23, 25, 28-32, 35, 46-51.

27. Stuart, *Life of Jonathan Trumbull*, pp. 620-621; Shipton, "Jonathan Trumbull," *loc. cit.*, p. 297.

28. Jonathan Trumbull to John Trumbull, November 1, 1784, Jonathan Trumbull, Sr., Papers, The Connecticut Historical Society, Box IV.

29. Jonathan Trumbull to John Trumbull, April 29, 1785, Jonathan Trumbull, Sr., Papers, The Connecticut Historical Society, Box IV.

30. John Trumbull did not return to the United States until 1789, some four years after the death of his father in August, 1785.

31. Quoted in Shipton, "Jonathan Trumbull," *loc. cit.*, pp. 285-286.

32. Quoted in Stuart, *Life of Jonathan Trumbull*, pp. 268-269.

33. Quoted in Stuart, *Life of Jonathan Trumbull*, p. 261.

34. Jonathan Trumbull to Roger Sherman, Eliphalet Dyer, and Silas Deane, November 7, 1775, Jonathan Trumbull, Sr., Papers, The Connecticut Historical Society, Box III.

35. Quoted in Stuart, *Life of Jonathan Trumbull*, pp. 272-273.

36. Stuart, *Life of Jonathan Trumbull*, p. 180.

37. Agnes Hunt, *The Provincial Committees of Safety of the American Revolution* (Cleveland, 1904), pp. 53-61.

38. Margaret Burnham Macmillan, *The War Governors in the American Revolution* (New York, 1943), pp. 124-125.

39. *Connecticut Colonial Records,* XIV, 432.

40. *Ibid.,* XV, 14.

41. Van Dusen, *Connecticut,* p. 161; Ralph V. Harlow, "Aspects of Revolutionary Finance, 1775-1783," *American Historical Review,* XXXV (October, 1929), p. 50.

42. E. James Ferguson, *The Power of the Purse: A History of American Public Finance, 1776-1790* (Chapel Hill, 1961), pp. 3-24; Van Dusen, *Connecticut,* p. 161.

43. Forrest Morgan, "Jonathan Trumbull—The Evolution of an Administrator," *Americana,* VII (March, 1921), p. 238.

44. Jonathan Trumbull to the Connecticut Delegation in Congress, December 8, 1778; Jonathan Trumbull to Henry Laurens, December 10, 1778, Trumbull Papers, *Massachusetts Historical Society Collections,* Seventh Series, II (1902), 318-320, 321-324.

45. Connecticut's taxes were extremely low throughout the Colonial Period. Henry Bronson, "Connecticut Currency, Continental Money, and the Finances of the Revolution," *New Haven Colony Historical Society Papers,* I (1865), pp. 30, 86-87.

46. Charles J. Hoadly *et al.* compliers, *The Public Records of the State of Connecticut, 1776-1784* (Hartford, 1894-), I, 139, Hereinafter cited as *Connecticut State Records.*

47. *Connecticut State Records,* I, 242, 377, 425.

48. Philip H. Jordan, Jr., "Connecticut Politics During the Revolution and the Confederation; 1776-1789" (Unpublished Dissertation, Yale University, 1962), pp. 102-109.

49. Stuart, *Life of Jonathan Trumbull,* p. 197.

50. *Connecticut Colonial Records,* XIV, 415-416; XV, 14-15, 119, 135, 314, 413; *Connecticut State Records,* I, 12, 63-64, 71, 123-124; II, 17, 222-223, 267-271, 450-452; III, 13-14, 39, 129, 519-520.

51. As New York prepared to meet the expected advance of British troops from Canada in the early months of 1777, Trumbull was urged by James Livingston, the chairman of the Committee of Safety for the State of New York, to repeal the Connecticut embargo, since a hardship was being worked upon New Yorkers. James Livingston to Jonathan Trumbull, January 14, 1777, Trumbull Papers, *Massachusetts Historical Society Collections,* Seventh Series, II (1902), 8-10. Trumbull responded to Livingston by noting that the Connecticut embargo was passed to make certain that the state's provisions would not fall into the hands of the enemies of America, *e.g.,* the British in New York City. Jonathan Trumbull to the New York Committee of Safety, January 22, 1777, Trumbull Papers, *Massachusetts Historical Society Collections,* Seventh Series, II (1902), 13-14. Schuyler entered the controversy at this time, writing to Trumbull that the Connecticut embargo has evoked great negative sentiment in New York and then asking if in fact such legislation existed! The implication, of course, that Connecticut could not have been responsible for such legislation hardly put Trumbull in a gleeful mood. Philip Schuyler to Jonathan Trumbull, January 23, 1777, Trumbull Papers, *Massachusetts Historical Society Collections,* Seventh Series, II (1902), 32-33.

52. Johnson, *The Administration of the American Commissariat During the Revolutionary War,* pp. 11, 15, 27.

53. *Connecticut Colonial Records,* XV, 15-16, 40.

54. Van Dusen, *Connecticut,* p. 158; *Connecticut State Records,* II, 132-133, 175-176, 521-526, 531, 541.

55. *Connecticut State Records,* II, 455-456.

56. Fitzpatrick, ed., *The Writings of George Washington,* XI, 442.

57. *Ibid.*, XI, 35, 417.

58. *Ibid.*, XI, 453.

59. George Washington to Jonathan Trumbull, March 31, 1778, Trumbull Papers, *Massachusetts Historical Society Collections,* Fifth Series, X (1888), 111-113.

60. John Richard Alden, *The American Revolution, 1775-1783* (New York, 1954), p. 197.

61. John Joseph Stoudt, *Ordeal at Valley Forge* (Philadelphia, 1963), *passim.*

62. Johnson, *The Administration of the American Commissariat During the Revolutionary War,* p. 93.

63. Fitzpatrick, ed., *The Writings of George Washington,* X, 267.

64. *Ibid.*, X, 469, 471, 482, 483.

65. George Washington to Jonathan Trumbull, February 6, 1778, Trumbull Papers, *Massachusetts Historical Society Collections,* Fifth Series, X (1888), 110-111.

66. *Connecticut State Records,* I, 571-572.

67. Stuart, *Life of Jonathan Trumbull,* p. 366.

68. *Ibid.*, p. 367.

69. Van Dusen, *Connecticut,* p. 159.

70. Quoted in Stuart, *Life of Jonathan Trumbull,* p. 367.

71. *Ibid.*, pp. 367-370.

72. Lynn Montross, *Rag, Tag and Bobtail: The Story of the Continental Army, 1775-1783* (New York, 1952), p. 347.

73. Quoted in Montross, *op. cit.*, pp. 347-348.

74. George Washington to Jonathan Trumbull, January 6, 1780, Trumbull Papers, *Massachusetts Historical Society Collections,* Fifth Series, X (1888), 152-153.

75. The anecdote was remembered by Washington's adopted son, George Washington Parke Custis, and in quoted in Stuart, *Life of Jonathan Trumbull,* p. 469.

76. Jonathan Trumbull to George Washington, March 10, 1780, Trumbull Papers, *Massachusetts Historical Society Collections,* Fifth Series, X (1888), 158-160.

77. Stuart, *Life of Jonathan Trumbull,* p. 469.

78. Johnson, *The Administration of the American Commissariat During the Revolutionary War,* pp. 160-161.

79. *Ibid.*, pp. 161-176, 191-197.

80. Carl Van Doren, *Mutiny in January* (New York, 1943), *passim.*

81. George Washington to Jonathan Trumbull, March 10, 1780; George Washington to Jonathan Trumbull, March 26, 1780; George Washington to Jonathan Trumbull, May 26, 1780; George Washington to Jonathan Trumbull, June 1, 1780; George Washington to Jonathan Trumbull, August 22, 1780; George Washington to Jonathan Trumbull, October 28, 1780; George Washington to Jonathan Trumbull, December 10, 1780; George Washington to Jonathan Trumbull, February 4, 1781; George Washington to Jonathan Trumbull, May 10, 1781, Trumbull Papers, *Massachusetts Historical Society Collections,* Fifth Series, X (1888), 158, 161-162, 165-166, 166-168, 197-198, 213-214, 217, 231-237.

82. *Connecticut State Records,* II, 510, 512.

83. *Ibid.*, III, 160.

84. *Ibid.*, III, 218, 221.

85. *Ibid.*, III, 381, 383; Stuart, *Life of Jonathan Trumbull,* pp. 517-527.

86. Quoted in Van Dusen, *Connecticut,* p. 161.

87. Jonathan Trumbull to George Washington, January 31, 1781, Trumbull Papers, *Massachusetts Historical Society Collections,* Fifth Series, X (1888), 230-231.

88. Jonathan Trumbull to George Washington, March 10, 1780, Trumbull Papers, *Massachusetts Historical Society Collections*, Fifth Series, X (1888), 158-160.

89. Johnson, *The Administration of the American Commissariat During the Revolutionary War*, p. 166.

90. Gaillard Hunt, Worthington C. Ford, John C. Fitzpatrick, and Roscoe R. Hill, eds., *Journals of the Continental Congress, 1774-1789* (34 vols: Washington, D.C., 1904-1937), XVII, 487.

91. George Washington to Jonathan Trumbull, June 10, 1780, Trumbull Papers, *Massachusetts Historical Society Collections*, Fifth Series, X (1888), 170-171.

92. Samuel Huntington to William Greene, June 5, 1780; George Washington to William Greene, June 10, 1780, John Russell Bartlett, ed., *Records of the Colony of Rhode Island and Providence Plantations in New England* (10 vols: Providence, 1856-1865), IX, 117, 149-150.

93. Jonathan Trumbull to William Greene, June 8, 1780, Rhode Island Archives, Letters to the Governor, 1731-1880 (54 vols.), XIV, 131.

94. Connecticut Archives, Revolutionary War, 1763-1789, First Series, XIX, 273; Johnson, *The Administration of the American Commissariat During the Revolutionary War*, p. 174.

95. Macmillan, *The War Governors in the American Revolution*, p. 212; Johnson, *The Administration of the American Commissariat During the Revolutionary War*, pp. 106-107.

96. See C. H. Van Tyne, "French Aid before the Alliance of 1778," *American Historical Review*, XXXI (October, 1925), 20-40.

97. *Connecticut State Records*, II, 55.

98. *Connecticut Colonial Records*, XI, 190.

99. Van Dusen, *Connecticut*, p. 148.

100. *Connecticut Colonial Records*, XI, 258.

101. *Connecticut State Records*, I, 133.

102. *Ibid.*, II, 34-35, 55, 129, 163, 168, 352, 436, 502.

103. *Ibid.*, II, 247.

104. *Connecticut Colonial Records*, XI, 40.

105. *Ibid.*, XI, 173.

106. *Connecticut State Records*, III, 389.

107. *Ibid.*, III, 556.

108. *Ibid.*, I, 454, 578, 582; II, 161.

109. *Connecticut Colonial Records*, XIV, 418, XV, 17-18, 127, 317-318, 323.

110. *Connecticut State Records*, I, 130.

111. *Ibid.*, I, 53.

112. *Ibid.*, I, 172, 179, 399, 403, 467, 518, 519.

113. *Ibid.*, I, 23.

114. *Ibid.*, I, 172.

115. *Ibid.*, I, 259; II, 542.

116. *Ibid.*, II, 163, 303, 352; III, 81, 85, 261.

117. Jonathan Trumbull to Philip Schuyler, January 3, 1777, Trumbull Papers, *Massachusetts Historical Society Collections*, Seventh Series, II (1902), 6-7; *Connecticut State Records*, I, 159.

118. *Connecticut State Records*, I, 155, 210, 216, 331, 332, 393; II, 98.

119. A detailed account of the Salisbury operation is Louis F. Middlebrook, *Salisbury Connecticut Cannon, Revolutionary War* (Salem, Massachusetts, 1935).

120. *Connecticut State Records*, I, 181, 240, 425; II, 280, 365; III, 30, 184, 378, 462.

121. "Rolls and Lists of Connecticut Men in the Revolution, 1775-1783," *Connecticut Historical Society Collections*, VIII (1901), *passim*.

122. Van Dusen, *Connecticut*, pp. 150-155.

123. Philip Schuyler to Jonathan Trumbull, October 12, 1775, Jonathan Trumbull, Sr., Papers, The Connecticut Historical Society, Box II.

124. Jonathan Trumbull to Eliphalet Dyer, Roger Sherman, and Silas Deane, December 9, 1775, Jonathan Trumbull, Sr., Papers, The Connecticut Historical Society, Box II.

125. Quoted in Van Dusen, *Connecticut*, p. 151.

126. *Connecticut State Records*, I, 25, 254.

127. See, for example, Jonathan Trumbull to George Washington, January 14, 1777; January 23, 1777; February 1, 1777, Trumbull Papers, *Massachusetts Historical Society Collections*, Fifth Series, X (1888), 24-26, 27-30, 34.

128. Jonathan Trumbull to George Washington, February 7, 1777, Trumbull Papers, *Massachusetts Historical Society Collections*, Fifth Series, X (1888), 35-38.

129. Van Dusen, *Connecticut*, p. 152.

130. Jordon, "Connecticut Politics During the Revolution and Confederation; 1776-1789," pp. 58-79.

131. *Connecticut Courant*, April 22, 1776.

132. *Connecticut Colonial Records*, XV, 415.

133. Forrest McDonald, *The Formation of the American Republic, 1776-1790* (Boston, 1965), pp. 6-9.

134. Quoted in Jordan, "Connecticut Politics During the Revolution and Confederation, 1776-1789," p. 60.

135. Merrill Jensen, *The Articles of Confederation: An Interpretation of the Social-Constitutional History of the American Revolution, 1774-1781* (Madison, Wisconsin, 1940), pp. 140-145.

136. Connecticut Archives, Revolutionary War, 1763-1789, First Series, XIII, 314abcde.

137. Jensen, *The Articles of Confederation*, pp. 145-146.

138. *Ibid.*, 249-270; Edmund C. Burnett, *The Continental Congress* (New York, 1941), pp. 237-240, 248-258.

139. Jonathan Trumbull to Roger Sherman, Titus Hosmer, and Andrew Adams, August 25, 1778, Trumbull Papers, *Massachusetts Historical Society Collections*, Seventh Series, II (1902), 256-257.

140. Jordan, "Connecticut Politics During the Revolution and Confederation, 1776-1789," pp. 62-64.

141. The Jonathan Trumbull Papers, Connecticut State Library, XXIX, 148.

142. *Connecticut State Records*, I, 467.

143. *Connecticut Courant*, December 23, 1777.

144. Jordan, *op. cit.*, pp. 64-65.

145. *Ibid.*, pp. 65-66.

146. *Ibid.*, pp. 65-66.

147. *Ibid.*, p. 67.

148. *Ibid.*, p. 70.

149. The Jonathan Trumbull Papers, Connecticut State Library, XX, 167b.

150. Allan Nevins, *The American States During and After the Revolution* (New York, 1924), p. 222.

151. Connecticut Archives, Revolutionary War, 1763-1789, First Series, X, 85b.

152. Jordan, *op. cit.*, pp. 70-71.

153. *Connecticut State Records*, I, 532-533.

154. *Ibid.*, I, 533. The General Assembly also considered the town desire to elect the state's congressional representatives. Trumbull supported this position until the General Assembly in May, 1779, finally gave its assent. See Jordan, "Connecticut Politics During the Revolution and Confederation, 1776-1789," pp. 74-76.

155. Jensen, *The Articles of Confederation*, pp. 194-195.

156. Jensen, *The Articles of Confederation*, pp. 198ff.; Burnett, *The Continental Congress*, pp. 217, 220, 222, 240, 341, 345, 493-494; Nevins, *The American States During and After the Revolution*, pp. 623-626.

157. Jonathan Trumbull to the Connecticut Delegation in Congress, February 22, 1779, Trumbull Papers, *Massachusetts Historical Society Collections*, Seventh Series, II (1902), 361-362.

158. *Connecticut State Records*, II, 231-232.

159. Jensen, *The Articles of Confederation*, pp. 225, 228, 236, 238.

160. *Connecticut State Records*, III, 177-178.

161. Hunt, *et al.*, *Journals of the Continental Congress, 1774-1789*, XX, 704.

162. Titus Hosmer to Jonathan Trumbull, August 31, 1778, Trumbull Papers, *Massachusetts Historical Society Collections*, Seventh Series, II (1902), 264-267.

163. Andrew Adams to Jonathan Trumbull, September 5, 1778, Trumbull Papers, *Massachusetts Historical Society Collections*, Seventh Series, II (1902), 268-270.

164. Jonathan Trumbull to the Connecticut Delegation in Congress, October 5, 1778, Trumbull Papers, *Massachusetts Historical Society Collections*, II (1902), 274-276.

165. Ferguson, *The Power of the Purse*, p. 51.

166. Roger Sherman to Jonathan Trumbull, November 24, 1778, Trumbull Papers, *Massachusetts Historical Society Collections*, Seventh Series, II (1902), 312.

167. Jonathan Trumbull to the Connecticut Delegation in Congress, December 8, 1778; Jonathan Trumbull to Henry Laurens, December 10, 1778; Jonathan Trumbull to Samuel Huntington, December 13, 1778, Trumbull Papers, *Massachusetts Historical Society Collections*, Seventh Series, II (1902), 318-320, 321-324, 458-460.

168. McDonald, *The Formation of the American Republic, 1776-1790*, p. 14.

169. *Ibid.*, p. 14.

170. Ferguson, *The Power of the Purse*, pp. 44-60.

171. McDonald, *The Formation of the American Republic, 1776-1790*, p. 14.

172. *Ibid.*, pp. 14-15.

173. *Ibid.*, p. 15.

174. *Ibid.*, p. 15; Ferguson, *The Power of the Purse*, pp. 50-69.

175. Burnett, *The Continental Congress*, pp. 480-481.

176. See Clarence L. Ver Steeg, *Robert Morris, Revolutionary Financier* (Philadelphia, 1954), pp. 92, 94ff.

WAR GOVERNOR: STATE AFFAIRS

1. An interesting evaluation of Trumbull's war governorship is Andrew M. Davis, "Trials of a Governor in the Revolution," *Massachusetts Historical Society Proceedings*, Second Series, XLVII (January, 1914), 131-141.

2. Margaret Burnham Macmillan, *The War Governors in the American Revolution* (New York, 1943), p. 26.

3. *Ibid.*, pp. 14-56.

4. *Ibid.*, p. 26; Nevins, *The American States During and After the American Revolution*, p. 164.

5. The following discussion of Connecticut government in the middle decades of the eighteenth century is based on Jordan, "Connecticut Politics During the Revolution and Confederation, 1776-1789," pp. 26-57.

6. Only three Connecticut governors in the eighteenth century left the office involuntarily: Roger Wolcott (1750-1754); Thomas Fitch (1754-1766); and Matthew Griswold (1784-1786).

7. Agnes Hunt, *The Provincial Committees of Safety of the American Revolution* (Cleveland, 1904), p. 151.

8. *Ibid.*, p. 53.

9. *Ibid.*, p. 9-150.

10. *Ibid.*, p. 154.

11. *Ibid.*, pp. 53-61.

12. *Connecticut State Records*, I, 37, 70, 73, 118, 373; Royal R. Hinman, compiler, *A Historical Collection from Official Records, Files, etc., of the Part Sustained by Connecticut During the War of the Revolution* (Hartford, 1842), p. 98.

13. Gold Selleck Silliman to Jonathan Trumbull, August 2, 1777; Thaddeus Burr to Jonathan Trumbull, July 4, 1777; Jedediah Huntington to Jonathan Trumbull, July 5, 1777; Oliver Wolcott to Jonathan Trumbull, July 9, 1777, Trumbull Papers, *Massachusetts Historical Society Collections*, Seventh Series, II (1902), 66-68, 68-69, 75, 98-102.

14. Jonathan Trumbull to George Washington, May 4, 1777; May 18, 1777; May 22, 1777, Trumbull Papers, *Massachusetts Historical Society Collections*, Fifth Series, X (1888), 59-61, 62-64, 64-65.

15. George Washington to Jonathan Trumbull, May 23, 1777; May 26, 1777, Trumbull Papers, *Massachusetts Historical Society Collections*, Fifth Series, X (1888), 65-67, 67-68.

16. Hunt, *The Provincial Committees of Safety of the American Revolution*, p. 56.

17. Jonathan Trumbull to George Washington, June 12, 1777, Trumbull Papers, *Massachusetts Historical Society Collections*, Fifth Series, X (1888), 70-71.

18. Gold Selleck Silliman to Jonathan Trumbull, April 24, 1778; William Ledyard to Jonathan Trumbull, December I, 1778; Samuel H. Parsons to Jonathan Trumbull, February 27, 1779; Selectmen of New Haven to Jonathan Trumbull, July 9, 1779; Samuel Mott to Jonathan Trumbull, August 20, 1779; Peter Colt to Jonathan Trumbull, December 16, 1779; John Bell to Jonathan Trumbull, August 30, 1780, Trumbull Papers, *Massachusetts Historical Society Collections*, Seventh Series, II (1902), 230-231, 313-314, 365-367, 377-379, 406, 422-423, 461-463; III (1902), 118-119.

19. Jonathan Trumbull to George Washington, October 28, 1778; George Washington to Jonathan Trumbull, November 12, 1779; George Washington to Jonathan Trumbull, November 20, 1779; George Washington to Jonathan Trumbull, June 14, 1780, Trumbull Papers, *Massachusetts Historical Society Collections*, Fifth Series, X (1888)', 129, 144-145, 147, 176.

20. While dispatches from Trumbull and the Committee of Safety in Lebanon regarding the raising of troops and the collection of arms and provisions for the Connecticut Militia make up a substantial portion of The Jonathan Trumbull Papers, Connecticut State Library, IV-XIV, *passim,* such material is also in other Trumbull collections. See, for example, Jonathan Trumbull to Shubael Griswold, January 18, 1776; Jonathan Trumbull to Nathaniel Buell, January 19, 1776; Jonathan Trumbull to Samuel Abbott, September 6, 1776; Jonathan Trumbull to the Stonington Selectmen, August 1, 1776; John Ely to Jonathan Trumbull, September 26, 1777; Selleck Silliman to Jonathan Trumbull, September 22, 1778; Jonathan Trumbull to John Tyler, October 6, 1779; Jonathan Trumbull to Nehemiah Hubbard, August 7, 1780; Jonathan Trumbull to Thomas Mumford, September 8, 1781, Jonathan Trumbull, Sr., Papers, The Connecticut Historical Society, Boxes III and IV. Jonathan Trumbull to Andrew Adams, September 13, 1780, Document HM22436, Henry E. Huntington Library and Art Gallery. Jonathan Trumbull to Jedediah Huntington, January 30, 1779, The Jonathan Trumbull Papers, Morristown National Historical Park. Jonathan Trumbull to

Jonathan Fitch, September 13, 1776, Emmett Collection, New York Public Library. Jonathan Trumbull to Woodstock Selectmen, August 1, 1776, Feinstone Collection, American Philosophical Society Library.

21. *Connecticut Colonial Records*, XV, 99-100.

22. The definitive study of Connecticut's naval efforts in the Revolutionary War is Louis F. Middlebrook, *History of Maritime Connecticut During the American Revolution, 1775-1783* (2 vols: Salem, Massachusetts, 1925).

23. See, for example, Jonathan Trumbull to Andrew and Joshua Huntington, August 20, 1776; Jonathan Trumbull to Timothy Parker, December 6, 1777; Samuel Brown to Jonathan Trumbull, April 1, 1779; Timothy Parker to Jonathan Trumbull, May 26, 1779, Jonathan Trumbull, Sr., Papers, The Connecticut Historical Society, Boxes III and IV.

24. *Connecticut Colonial Records*, XV, 474; *Connecticut State Records*, II, 136.

25. Samuel Eliot, Jr., to Jonathan Trumbull, August 3, 1778; August 6, 1778; September 14, 1778, Trumbull Papers, *Massachusetts Historical Society Collections*, Seventh Series, II (1902), 243-244, 246, 271-272.

26. Samuel Eliot, Jr., to Jonathan Trumbull, October 2, 1778, Trumbull Papers, *Massachusetts Historical Society Collections*, Seventh Series, II (1902), 272-273.

27. Andrew Eliot to Jonathan Trumbull, June 5, 1777; Samuel Eliot, Jr., to Jonathan Trumbull, January 22, 1779, Trumbull Papers, *Massachusetts Historical Society Collections*, Seventh Series, II (1902), 53-54, 333-334.

28. Samuel Eliot, Jr., to Jonathan Trumbull, March 13, 1781, Trumbull Papers, *Massachusetts Historical Society Collections*, Seventh Series, II (1902),

29. Middlebrook, *History of Maritime Connecticut During the American Revolution*, I, 80-86.

30. *Ibid.*, I, 42-45, 48-54.

31. *Ibid.*, I, 204.

32. Van Dusen, *Connecticut*, pp. 156-157.

33. The Connecticut fleet was occasionally used by Trumbull to carry dispatches to Europe by request of Congress. See, for example, Richard Henry Lee and James Lovell to Jonathan Trumbull, May 19, 1778, Trumbull Papers, *Massachusetts Historical Society Collections*, Seventh Series, II (1902), 234.

34. Burnett, *The Continental Congress*, pp. 139-140; Hunt, *et al.*, *Journals of the Continental Congress, 1774-1789*, III, 372-375; IV, 251-254.

35. *Connecticut Colonial Records*, XV, 280-281.

36. The owners and crew took one-half of the proceeds from a prize and the state the other half. County courts in Connecticut had jurisdiction over all cases involving prizes. Van Dusen, *Connecticut*, p. 157.

37. Van Dusen, *Connecticut*, pp. 157-158; Middlebrook, *History of Maritime Connecticut During the American Revolution*, I, 10; II, 51-52.

38. Van Dusen, *Connecticut*, p. 157.

39. See, for example, Jonathan Trumbull's signed commissions for the following Connecticut privateers: *Nancy*, October 5, 1776; *American Revenue*, June 15, 1776; *Fairfield*, May 13, 1777; *General Washington*, July 25, 1777; *Adams*, July 30, 1777, Jonathan Trumbull, Sr., Papers, The Connecticut Historical Society, Boxes III and IV.

40. Van Dusen, *Connecticut*, p. 158.

41. See Edgar S. Maclay, *History of American Privateers* (New York, 1899), *passim*, and Montross, *Rag, Tag and Bobtail: The Story of the Continental Army, 1775-1783*, pp. 85, 147, 327, 338, 340.

42. See especially Jonathan Trumbull to Matthew Griswold, October 5, 1775, and Jonathan Trumbull to Jeremiah Wadsworth, November 19, 1780,

Jonathan Trumbull, Sr., Papers, The Connecticut Historical Society, Boxes III and IV.

43. Quoted in Forrest Morgan, "Jonathan Trumbull—The Evolution of an Administrator," *Americana*, VII (March, 1912), 247-248.

44. *Ibid.*, p. 250.

45. Zeichner, *Connecticut's Years of Controversy*, pp. 200-204.

46. *Ibid.*, pp. 203-204.

47. The Jonathan Trumbull Papers, Connecticut State Library, XX, 116ab.

48. Zeichner, *Connecticut's Years of Controversy*, pp. 205-206.

49. *Ibid.*, p. 207.

50. *Ibid.*, p. 207.

51. The Jonathan Trumbull Papers, Connecticut State Library, XX, Part 1, 119a.

52. *Connecticut Colonial Records*, XV, 192-195; Zeichner, *Connecticut's Years of Controversy*, pp. 207-208; Van Dusen, *Connecticut*, p. 143; The Jonathan Trumbull Papers, Connecticut State Library, XXIX, 37.

53. *Connecticut State Records*, I, 7-8, 27-28.

54. Zeichner, *Connecticut's Years of Controversy*, pp. 233-234.

55. Epaphroditus Peck, *The Loyalists of Connecticut*, Tercentenary Commission of the State of Connecticut, *Pamphlet* Number 31 (New Haven, 1934), p. 28.

56. *Connecticut State Records*, I, 254.

57. It has to be noted that in May, 1778, the Connecticut General Assembly did pass an extremely harsh act providing for the confiscation of Tory property. *Connecticut State Records*, II, 279-280. This legislation, however, was aimed not so much at the individual who was identified as possessing Loyalist views, but at those Connecticut Tories who took up arms against the state and the nation by serving in British regiments organized in New York. The Connecticut authorities were not inclined to offer sympathetic treatment to these Tories, some of whom had participated in the 1777 attack on Danbury. See Peck, *op. cit.*, p. 22.

58. Oliver Ellsworth to Jonathan Trumbull, September 28, 1779, Jonathan Trumbull, Sr., Papers, The Connecticut Historical Society, Box IV.

59. Oliver Wolcott to Jonathan Trumbull, July 3, 1781, Trumbull Papers, *Massachusetts Historical Society Collections*, Seventh Series, III (1902), 234-236.

60. Peck, *The Loyalists of Connecticut*, pp. 20-21.

61. Ebenezer Punderson to Jonathan Trumbull, October 13, 1778, Trumbull Papers, *Massachusetts Historical Society Collections*, Seventh Series, II (1902), 287.

62. Titus Hosmer to Jonathan Trumbull, Febuary 24, 1779, Trumbull Papers, *Massachusetts Historical Society Collections*, Seventh Series, II (1902), 364.

63. Matthew Graves to Jonathan Trumbull, August 4, 1779, Trumbull Papers, *Massachusetts Historical Society Collections*, Seventh Series, II (1902), 416.

64. Bela Hubbard to Jonathan Trumbull, July 24, 1780, Trumbull Papers, *Massachusetts Historical Society Collections*, Seventh Series, III (1902), 93-94.

65. Jonathan Trumbull to Samuel Wadsworth, July 22, 1775; Lynde Lorde to Jonathan Trumbull, August 1, 1777; James Hamilton to Jonathan Trumbull, August 2, 1781, Jonathan Trumbull, Sr., Papers, The Connecticut Historical Society, Boxes III and IV. William Heath to Jonathan Trumbull, November 2, 1778, Jacob Gerrish to Jonathan Trumbull, November 10, 1778; Thomas Seymour to Jonathan Trumbull, November 18, 1778, Trumbull Papers, *Massachusetts Historical Society Collections*, Seventh Series, II (1902), 301-302, 307, 311.

66. Shipton, "Jonathan Trumbull," *loc. cit.*, pp. 291-292.

67. Shipton, "Jonathan Trumbull," *loc. cit.*, p. 292. On Trumbull's efforts at exchanging prisoners, see Jonathan Trumbull to Ezekiel Williams, July 16, 1777;

Selectmen of Norwalk to Jonathan Trumbull, May 5, 1778; Stephen St. John to Jonathan Trumbull, October 30, 1779, Jonathan Trumbull, Sr., Papers, The Connecticut Historical Society, Box IV.

68. Town of Wethersfield to Jonathan Trumbull, July 19, 1780, Trumbull Papers, *Massachusetts Historical Society Collections*, Seventh Series, III (1902), 69-74.

69. Selectmen of Plymouth to Jonathan Trumbull, February 15, 1779; Isaac Lathrop to Jonathan Trumbull, February 15, 1779; James Warren to Jonathan Trumbull, February 20, 1779, Trumbull Papers, *Massachusetts Historical Society Collections*, Seventh Series, II (1902), 357-358, 359-360, 360-361.

70. Nathaniel Coffin to Jonathan Trumbull, January 26, 1779, Trumbull Papers, *Massachusetts Historical Society Collections*, Seventh Series, II (1902), 337.

71. William Greene to Jonathan Trumbull, January 20, 1779; Peleg Clarke and Nathaniel Mumford to the Connecticut General Assembly, January 23, 1779, Trumbull Papers, *Massachusetts Historical Society Collections*, Seventh Series, II (1902), 334-336.

72. Forrest Morgan, "Jonathan Trumbull—The Evolution of an Administrator," *loc. cit.*, p. 248.

73. Quotation cited in Shipton, "Jonathan Trumbull," *loc. cit.*, p. 292.

74. Jordan, "Connecticut Politics During the Revolution and Confederation; 1776-1789," p. 110.

75. Macmillan, *The War Governors in the American Revolution*, pp. 151-154.

76. William Williams to Jonathan Trumbull, March 29, 1780, The Jonathan Trumbull Papers, Connecticut State Library, XI, 122.

77. George Washington to Jonathan Trumbull, April 12, 1777; Jonathan Trumbull to John Tyler, August 27, 1779; Jonathan Trumbull to George Washington, December 27, 1779; George Washington to Jonathan Trumbull, January 14, 1780; Jonathan Trumbull to George· Clinton, July 20, 1781, Trumbull Papers, *Massachusetts Historical Society Collections*, Fifth Series, X (1888), 55-56, 149-151, 154-155; Seventh Series, II (1902), 428-429; III (1902), 248-251.

78. Jonathan Trumbull to the Connecticut General Assembly, January 29, 1782, Jonathan Trumbull, Sr., Papers, The Connecticut Historical Society, Box IV.

79. Connecticut Archives, Revolutionary War, 1763-1789, First Series, XXII, 85-86, The Jonathan Trumbull Papers, Connecticut State Library, XX, 342.

80. Shipton, "Jonathan Trumbull," *loc. cit.*, p. 295.

81. Jordan, "Connecticut Politics During the Revolution and Confederation, 1776-1789," p. 84.

82. Albert E. Van Dusen, "The Trade of Revolutionary Connecticut" (Unpublished Dissertation, University of Pennsylvania, 1948), pp. 330-334, 340, 346, 375-376.

83. Jordan, "Connecticut Politics During the Revolution and Confederation, 1776-1789," pp. 85-86.

84. The Connecticut General Assembly attempted throughout the war to establish price regulations. However, the inability to secure cooperation from neighboring states doomed the attempt to failure.

85. Jordan, "Connecticut Politics During the Revolution and Confederation, 1776-1789," pp. 104-105.

86. *Ibid.*, p. 106.

87. *Ibid.*, pp. 106-109.

88. *Ibid.*, pp. 115-119.

89. Merrill Jensen, *The New Nation: A History of the United States During the Confederation, 1781-1789* (New York, 1950), p. 72.

90. Douglas Southall Freeman, *George Washington: A Biography* (7 vols: New York, 1948-1957), V, 431-437.

91. Hunt, *et al.*, *Journals of the Continental Congress, 1774-1789*, XXIV, 145-150, 207-209.

92. Jordan, "Connecticut Politics During the Revolution and Confederation, 1776-1789," pp. 136-137.

93. *Ibid.*, pp. 141-146.

94. The agrarians met at Middletown in September, 1783, to protest against commutation and to lay plans for the electoral defeat of the nationalist-oriented members of the Council, *i.e.*, Oliver Wolcott, Eliphalet Dyer, Oliver Ellsworth, Abraham Davenport, Benjamin Huntington, and Roger Sherman. See Jordan, *op. cit.*, pp. 158-160.

95. Jordan, "Connecticut Politics During the Revolution and Confederation, 1776-1789," pp. 98-100.

96. *Ibid.*, pp. 111-112.

97. *Ibid.*, pp. 106-109.

98. *Ibid.*, pp. 89-94.

99. *Ibid.*, pp. 103-106.

100. Jeremiah Wadsworth to Jonathan Trumbull, March 31, 1780, Jeremiah Wadsworth Papers, The Connecticut Historical Society, Box 130.

101. Jordan, "Connecticut Politics During the Revolution and Confederation, 1776-1789," pp. 114-119; Shipton, "Jonathan Trumbull," *loc. cit.*, p. 296.

102. Stuart, *Life of Jonathan Trumbull*, pp. 600-601; Jonathan Trumbull to Jonathan Trumbull, Jr., June 7, 1783, The Jonathan Trumbull Papers, Connecticut State Library, XX, 354,

103. Jordan, "Connecticut Politics During the Revolution and Confederation, 1776-1789," pp. 135-157.

104. Trumbull's speech to the General Assembly is reprinted in full in Stuart, *Life of Jonathan Trumbull*, pp. 604-608.

105. *Connecticut State Records*, V, 219.

106. Jordan, "Connecticut Politics During the Revolution and Confederation, 1776-1789," p. 219.

107. *Ibid.*, pp. 219-220.

108. *Connecticut State Records*, V, 326-327.

109. The memorial is reprinted in Stuart, *Life of Jonathan Trumbull*, pp. 649-650.

110. Stuart, *Life of Jonathan Trumbull*, pp. 651-652.

RETIREMENT

1. P. Penet to Jonathan Trumbull, December 20, 1782; Comble and Company to Jonathan Trumbull, June 1, 1783; John De Neufville to Jonathan Trumbull, July 12, 1784, Jonathan Trumbull, Sr., Papers, The Connecticut Historical Society, Box IV.

2. Jonathan Trumbull to Lane, Son, and Fraser, April 20, 1783; Jonathan Trumbull to Champion and Hayley, April 20, 1783, Jonathan Trumbull, Sr., Papers, The Connecticut Historical Society, Box IV.

3. Champion and Dickason to Jonathan Trumbull, June 30, 1783, Jonathan Trumbull, Sr., Papers, The Connecticut Historical Society, Box IV.

4. Lane, Son, and Fraser to Jonathan Trumbull, July 28, 1783, Jonathan Trumbull, Sr., Papers, The Connecticut Historical Society, Box IV.

5. Lane, Son, and Fraser to Jonathan Trumbull, February 15, 1785, Jonathan Trumbull, Sr., Papers, The Connecticut Historical Society, Box IV.

6. Jonathan Trumbull to John Trumbull, April 29, 1785, Jonathan Trumbull, Sr., Papers, The Connecticut Hictorical Society, Box IV.

7. Stuart, *Life of Jonathan Trumbull*, p. 660.

8. *Ibid.*, p. 654n.

9. Weaver, *Jonathan Trumbull*, p. 150.

10. Ezra Stiles to Jonathan Trumbull, July 24, 1784, Jonathan Trumbull, Sr., Papers, The Connecticut Historical Society, Box IV.

11. Jonathan Trumbull to Ezra Stiles, August 19, 1784, Jonathan Trumbull, Sr., Papers, The Connecticut Historical Society, Box IV.

12. Ezra Stiles to Jonathan Trumbull, December [2], 1779, Jonathan Trumbull, Sr., Papers, The Connecticut Historical Society, Box IV.

13. Shipton, "Jonathan Trumbull," *loc. cit.*, p. 297.

14. Ezra Stiles to Jonathan Trumbull, February 26, 1783, Trumbull Papers, *Massachusetts Historical Society Collections*, Seventh Series, III (1902), 404.

15. Quotation cited in Stuart, *Life of Jonathan Trumbull*, pp. 581-582.

16. *Ibid.*, p. 582.

17. *Ibid.*, p. 582.

18. Anne-Cesar de la Luzerne to Jonathan Trumbull, September 24, 1779; The Comte De Rochambeau to Jonathan Trumbull, December 15, 1781, Trumbull Papers, *Massachusetts Historical Society Collections*, Seventh Series, II (1902), 439-440; III (1902), 304.

19. "Trumbull and Washington Letters," Trumbull Papers, *Massachusetts Historical Society Collections*, Fifth Series, X (1888), 1-281; The Jonathan Trumbull Papers, Connecticut State Library, XXV, *passim*.

20. Jonathan Trumbull to George Washington, June 10, 1783, Trumbull Papers, *Massachusetts Historical Society Collections*, Fifth Series, X (1888), 280-281.

21. Quotation cited in Shipton, "Jonathan Trumbull," *loc. cit.*, p. 296.

22. *Ibid.*, pp. 296-297.

23. The praise lavished upon Jonathan Trumbull was even more effusive after his death. A number of the euologies and sermons are quoted in Stuart, *Life of Jonathan Trumbull*, pp. 668-680.

24. Jonathan Trumbull to Henry Laurens, October 5, 1783, Jonathan Trumbull, Sr., Papers, The Connecticut Historical Society, Box IV.

25. Quotation cited in Stuart, *Life of Jonathan Trumbull*, pp. 667-668.